KB058303

거의 모든 **행동**
표현의 영어

서영조

한국외국어대학교 영어과, 동국대학교 대학원 연극영화과를 졸업했다.
영어 교재 출판 분야에서 유익한 영어 학습 콘텐츠를 개발해 왔고, 전문 번역가로서
영어권 도서들과 부산국제영화제를 비롯한 여러 영화제 출품작들을 번역하고 있다.
저서로《여행 영어의 결정적 패턴들》,《거의 모든 행동 표현의 일본어》,《영어 회화의 결정적 단어들》,
《영어 문장의 결정적 패턴들》,《디즈니 OST 잉글리시》,《디즈니 주니어 잉글리시 - 겨울왕국》,
《디즈니 주니어 잉글리시 - 토이 스토리 4》,《디즈니 영어 명대사 따라 쓰기》 등이 있고,
번역서로《브레인 룰스》,《조이풀》,《철학을 권하다》,《일생에 한 번은 가고 싶은 여행지 500》,
《거의 모든 영어의 구두법》 등이 있다.

거의 모든 행동 표현의 영어

지은이 서영조
초판 1쇄 발행 2022년 3월 10일
초판 13쇄 발행 2024년 6월 13일

발행인 박효상   **편집장** 김현   **기획 · 편집** 장경희, 이한경   **디자인** 임정현
본문 · 표지디자인 고희선   **편집 진행** 최주연
마케팅 이태호, 이전희   **관리** 김태옥

종이 월드페이퍼   **인쇄 · 제본** 예림인쇄 · 바인딩

출판등록 제10-1835호   **발행처** 사람in   **주소** 04034 서울시 마포구 양화로 11길 14-10 (서교동) 3F
전화 02) 338-3555(代)   **팩스** 02) 338-3545   **E-mail** saramin@netsgo.com
Website www.saramin.com

ISBN
978-89-6049-937-9 14740
978-89-6049-936-2 세트

우아한 지적만보, 기민한 실사구시 사람in

거의 모든 행동 표현의 영어

이런 행동은 영어로 뭐라고 하지?

궁금증이 시원하게 풀립니다!

스쿼트를 하다
DO SQUATS

커피를 내리다
brew coffee

옷을 수선하다
alter [mend] clothes

| pick the vegetables in the kitchen garden and make a salad.

시선 [눈길]을 돌리다
avert [turn away] one's eyes, look away

채소를 따다, 뜯다
PICK THE VEGETABLES

유튜브 영상을 보다

밀당하다, 튕기다
play hard to get

후진하다
BACK ONE'S CAR

watch a YouTube video, watch a video on YouTube

FOR ACTION

서영조 지음,

사람in

이런 행동은 영어로 어떻게 표현할까?

영어를 처음 배우는 아이들은 궁금한 것이 참 많습니다. 눈에 보이는 모든 것을 영어로는 뭐라고 하는지 알고 싶어 합니다. 사물의 이름을 영어로 배우고 나면 동작을 영어로 어떻게 표현하는지 궁금해합니다. 예를 들어 '코를 후비다', '팔을 뻗다' 같은 동작을 영어로 뭐라고 하는지 알고 싶어 하지요. 영어를 보통 십 년 넘게 학습한 성인들은 어떨까요? 그들에게 '코를 후비다', '팔을 뻗다'를 영어로 어떻게 표현하는지 물으면 얼른 대답하지 못할 것입니다. 어려운 영어 단어들은 많이 아는데, 정작 일상의 행동들은 쉬운 것도 영어로 잘 표현하지 못하는 경우가 많습니다.

이 책은 바로 그런 일상의 행동들을 영어로 어떻게 표현하는지 알려 주는 책입니다. 그런데 '영어 행동 표현들을 따로 배워야 하나?' 하고 생각하는 분들이 계실지도 모릅니다. 그 의문에 바로 답하자면 '그렇습니다.'입니다. 행동 표현들은 영어 회화, 즉 영어로 하는 대화의 많은 부분을 차지합니다. 우리가 같은 한국인들끼리 어떤 대화를 주고받는지 생각해 보세요. 아침에 출근해서는 어제 잠이 안 와 뒤척였다거나, 지하철을 놓쳤다거나 하는 말을 합니다. 주말에 뭐 했냐는 대화를 하면서는 넷플릭스로 영화를 봤다거나, 캠핑을 다녀왔다거나 하는 얘기를 나누죠. 친구의 전화를 받으면서는 지금 빨래를 널고 있었다거나, TV를 보며 저녁을 먹고 있었다고 말합니다. 모두 행동을 표현하는 말들입니다.

대화하는 동료나 친구가 외국인이어도 마찬가지입니다. 하는 말이 한국어에서 영어로 바뀔 뿐 내용은 크게 다르지 않습니다. 그러니 영어 회화를 잘하려면 우리가 하는 행동을 영어로 자유롭게 표현할 수 있어야 합니다. 이 책은 그런 영어 행동 표현들을 한데 모아 두어 여러분에게 지름길을 제시하는 책입니다.

사람들은 자신에게 친근한 것을 기반으로 학습할 때 새로운 내용을 쉽게 받아들이고 그다음 단계로 나아갈 수 있습니다. 영어 단어를 학습할 때는 자기 주변의 일상적인 단어들부터 점차 고급 어휘로 범위를 넓혀 갑니다. 영어 회화도 자신에게 익숙하고 친근한 내용부터 시작해서 점차 추상적인 내용으로 나아가야 합니다. 평생 한 번 쓸까 말까 한 내용은 나중으로 미루고, 피부에 와 닿는 익숙하고 일상적인 '행동'들을 영어로 표현하는 것부터 시작하는 게 바람직합니다.

대부분의 사람들이 영어를 잘하고 싶어 합니다. 영어를 잘한다는 건 여러 기준이 있을 수 있지만, 가장 기본은 하고 싶은 말을 막히지 않고 잘하는 것일 겁니다. 이 또한 다양한 영어 행동 표현을 알아야 하는 이유가 됩니다. 내가 했던, 내가 하는, 내가 할 '행동'을 영어로 명확하게 표현할 수 있다면 한 단계 높은 회화의 세계로 나아갈 기초는 마련된 것입니다.

이런 점들에 입각하여 《거의 모든 행동 표현의 영어》는 영어 회화의 기초가 될 수 있는 표현들을 크게 '신체 부위 행동 표현', '일상생활 속 행동 표현', '사회생활 속 행동 표현'으로 나누어 그림과 함께 제시합니다. 친숙한 표현들과 그에 맞는 그림들은 공부한다는 부담 없이 내용을 쉽게 받아들이고 기억하게 해 줄 것입니다. 그림을 넘겨보는 재미에 '아, 이런 행동은 영어로 이렇게 표현하는구나!' '아, 이런 행동까지 영어로 표현해 놨네?' 하는 감탄이 더해질 것입니다.

지금까지 끝까지 본 영어책이 없었다면 이 책을 끝까지 보는 걸 목표로 해 보세요. 하나하나 다 외우겠다는 부담이나 욕심은 버리세요. 이 페이지 저 페이지 관심 가는 곳을 펼쳐 보면서 학습하세요. 궁금한 표현이 있으면 인덱스에서 찾아보세요. 그렇게 학습하다 보면 어느새 많은 영어 행동 표현들이 여러분의 것이 되어 있는 걸 발견하실 겁니다.
여러분의 영어 학습을 응원합니다!

이 책은 총 3부, 17장으로 이루어져 있습니다. PART 1은 우리의 신체 부위를 이용한 행동 표현을, PART 2는 일상생활 속 행동 표현을, PART 3는 사회생활 속 행동 표현을 다루고 있습니다.

이 책은 반드시 처음부터 끝까지 보아야 하는 책은 아닙니다. 물론 앞에서부터 차근차근 학습하는 게 좋은 분들은 그렇게 하셔도 좋습니다. 하지만 그렇게 하지 않아도 됩니다. 목차를 보고 눈길이 가는 부분이나 어떤 내용일지 궁금한 부분을 펼쳐서 먼저 공부하고, 또 다른 궁금한 부분으로 넘어가서 학습하면 됩니다. 그리고 영어로 궁금한 표현이 있다면 언제든 인덱스에서 찾아보면 되고요.

첫술에 배부를 수 없다는 건 영어 공부에서도 절대적인 진리입니다. 이 책은 한 번 읽었다고 끝이 아니라 여러 번 반복해서 읽어야 합니다. 이미 알고 있는 표현이라면 확인만 하고 넘어가고, 모르던 표현일 경우에는 여러 번 반복해 읽어서 자기 것으로 만들어야 합니다. 이때 머릿속으로만 읽지 말고 입으로 소리 내어 읽는 게 훨씬 효과적입니다.

추천하는 학습 방법은 각각의 한글 표현을 읽고 영어로는 어떻게 말할지 생각해 본 다음 책에 나와 있는 영어 표현을 확인해 보는 것입니다. 학습이 어느 정도 이루어졌다는 생각이 들면 인덱스에 있는 한글 표현을 보면서 영어로 말해 보고, 영어 표현을 보면서 우리말 뜻을 말해 보는 훈련을 하세요. 영어 행동 표현을 온전히 자기 것으로 만드는 과정이 될 것입니다.

영어 회화 실력 향상에 꼭 필요한《거의 모든 행동 표현의 영어》는 다음과 같이 구성되어 있습니다.

본문의 영어 표현과 SENTENCES TO USE의 영어 문장을 원어민이 정확한 발음으로 녹음했습니다.

본문은 우리말–영어 표현 순으로 제시됩니다. 표현에서 take a hot/cold shower처럼 /는 take a hot shower, take a cold shower처럼 같은 위치의 단어를 해당 단어로 대체하면 다른 의미의 표현이 된다는 뜻입니다.

soak in a[the] bath는 soak in a bath, soak in the bath로 다른 단어를 대입해도 의미가 변하지 않는 걸 의미합니다. 이 경우, soak in a bath 하나만 녹음했습니다.

SENTENCES TO USE는 위에서 배운 표현이 실제 회화 문장에서 쓰이는 예를 보여줍니다.

어느 정도 학습이 되었다고 판단되면 인덱스의 한글 부분을 보면서 영어 표현을, 영어 부분을 보면서 우리말 표현을 말해 보세요. 이렇게 하면 여러분의 어휘 실력이 몰라볼 만큼 성장할 것입니다.

PART 2 일상생활 속 행동 표현

PART 3 사회생활 속 행동 표현

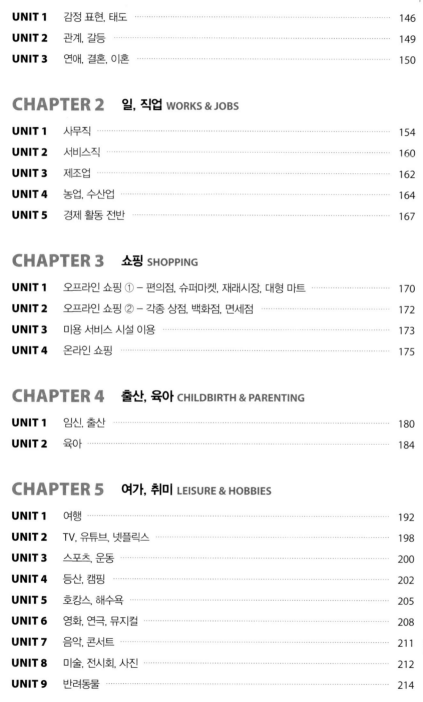

CHAPTER 1 감정 표현, 인간관계 EMOTIONS & RELATIONSHIP

CHAPTER 2 일, 직업 WORKS & JOBS

CHAPTER 3 쇼핑 SHOPPING

CHAPTER 4 출산, 육아 CHILDBIRTH & PARENTING

CHAPTER 5 여가, 취미 LEISURE & HOBBIES

PART I

신체 부위

행동 표현

CHAPTER

1

얼굴

FACE

1 고개(head)

MP3 001

고개를 들다
raise[lift] one's head

고개를 숙이다[떨구다]
lower one's head

고개를 끄덕이다
nod one's head

고개를 젓다
shake one's head

(~ 쪽으로) 고개를 돌리다
turn one's
head (toward(s) ~)

고개를 뒤로 젖히다
tilt one's head
back(wards)

고개를 기울이다
(뒤로, 앞으로, 왼쪽/오른쪽으로)
tilt one's head (back(wards), forward,
to the left/right)

고개를 까닥거리다
bob
one's head

고개를 갸웃하다
cock
one's head

고개를 내밀다
stick
one's head out

SENTENCES TO USE

고개를 들고 심호흡을 해.
Raise your head and take a deep breath.

그의 설명을 들으며 그녀는 천천히 고개를 끄덕였다.
Listening to his explanation, she nodded her head slowly.

우리는 소리가 나는 쪽으로 고개를 돌렸다.
We turned our heads towards the sound.

그녀는 고개를 뒤로 젖히고 얼굴로 비를 느꼈다.
She tilted her head back and felt the rain on her face.

아이는 문 밖으로 고개를 내밀었다.
The child stuck his head out the door.

2 머리(head, brain)

MP3 002

머리를 숙이다, 머리 숙여 인사하다
**bow
one's head**

* scratch one's head에는 '골똘히 생각하다, 어려운 문제의 해결책을 찾다'라는 뜻도 있다.

(난처하여) 머리를 긁다
**scratch
one's head**

머리를 쓰다듬다
**pat someone on the head,
stroke one's hair**

머리를 때리다
**hit someone
on the head**

머리를 다치다
**hurt one's head,
get hurt on the head,
have a head injury**

* 주로 don't bother your head about ~ 의 형태로 쓰인다.

(~에 대해) 걱정하다
**bother one's head
(about ~)**

머리를 쓰다[굴리다]
**use one's brain,
put one's brain to work**

머리를 쥐어짜다
**rack one's
brain(s)**

SENTENCES TO USE

그 정치가는 모여 있는 시민들에게 머리를 숙였다.	The politician bowed his head to the crowd of citizens.
그는 할 말을 찾지 못하고 머리를 긁적였다.	He scratched his head, unable to find anything to say.
그녀는 아이의 머리를 쓰다듬었다.	She patted the child on the head.
그는 그 교통사고로 머리를 다쳤다.	He hurt his head in the car accident.
그러지 말고 머리를 좀 써.	Come on, use your brain.

MP3 **003**

머리를 감다
wash[shampoo]
one's hair,
have a shampoo

머리를 헹구다
rinse one's hair

**수건으로 머리를
감싸다**
wrap one's hair
in a towel

머리를 말리다
dry one's hair

머리를 빗다
comb[brush]
one's hair

머리를 자르다[깎다]
have[get] one's hair
cut, have[get]
a haircut

머리를 박박 깎다
have[get] one's hair
shaved off, have[get]
one's head shaved

머리를 다듬다
have[get] one's
hair trimmed

머리를 퍼머하다
have[get] one's
hair permed,
have a perm

머리를 염색하다

(직접)
dye one's
hair

(다른 사람이)
get[have] one's
hair dyed

머리를 손질하다

(직접)
do one's
hair

(미용실에서)
get[have] one's
hair done

흰머리를 뽑다
pull out [pluck, tweeze,
remove] a gray hair

SENTENCES TO USE

자기 전에 머리를 잘 말리세요.

Dry your hair well before you go to bed.

그는 새로 생긴 미용실에서 머리를 깎았다.

He had his hair cut at the new hair salon.

우리 엄마는 한 달에 한 번 머리를 염색한다.

My mom dyes her hair once a month.

저녁에 데이트가 있어서 머리를 손질하고 있어.

I'm doing my hair since I have a date this evening.

머리를 기르다
grow out one's
hair, let one's
hair grow

머리를 뒤로 묶다
tie[put] one's
hair back

머리를 포니테일로 묶다
(동작)
tie[put] one's hair
in(to) a ponytail

포니테일 머리를 하다 (상태)
wear a ponytail,
have[wear] one's
hair in a ponytail

머리를 땋다
braid
one's hair

머리를 틀어 올리다
do one's hair up,
make a bun

머리를 풀다
let one's hair
down

(왼쪽/오른쪽으로) 가르마를 타다
part one's hair
(to[on] the left/right)

머리를 헝클다
mess up
one's hair

(절망이나 괴로움으로)
머리를 쥐어뜯다
tear one's hair out

머리가 빠지다
lose (one's) hair,
hair falls out

머리를 심다
get a hair
transplant

SENTENCES TO USE

머리를 길러 볼까 생각 중이에요.	I'm thinking about growing out my hair.
그 소녀는 고무줄로 머리를 뒤로 묶었다.	The girl tied her hair back with a rubber band.
그 여성은 포니테일을 하고 있었다.	The woman was wearing a ponytail.
그는 보통 왼쪽으로 가르마를 탄다.	He usually parts his hair to the left.
그는 어떻게 해야 할지 몰라 머리카락을 쥐어뜯었다.	Not knowing what to do, he tore his hair out.
최근에 머리가 너무 많이 빠진다.	I've been losing too much hair lately.

4 이마(forehead), 눈썹(eyebrow)

MP3 004

이마

이마를 찡그리다
wrinkle one's
forehead

이마의 땀을 닦다
wipe the sweat
off one's forehead

이마를 두드리다
tap one's
forehead

(열이 있는지) 이마를 짚어 보다
feel one's[someone's] forehead
(to see if one[someone] has a fever)

이마를 탁 치다
slap one's
forehead

이마를 맞대(고 의논하)다
put our/your/ their
heads together

눈썹

(족집게로) 눈썹을 뽑다
pluck[pull out]
one's eyebrows
(with tweezers)

눈살을 찌푸리다
frown,
knit one's
(eye)brows

(당황, 놀람, 경멸의 의미로)
눈썹을 치켜 올리다
raise one's
eyebrows

눈썹을 그리다
draw on
one's eyebrows

눈썹을 밀다
shave (off)
one's
eyebrows

SENTENCES TO USE

이마 찡그리지 마. 주름살 생겨.
Don't wrinkle your forehead. You'll get permanent wrinkles.

그는 손등으로 이마의 땀을 닦았다.
He wiped the sweat off his forehead with the back of his hand.

그녀는 열이 있는지 보려고 아이의 이마를 짚어 보았다.
She felt her child's forehead to see if he had a fever.

그들의 행동에 눈살을 찌푸리지 않을 수 없었다.   I couldn't help but frown at their behavior.

그녀는 아침마다 눈썹을 그린다.   She draws on her eyebrows every morning.

5 눈(eye), 코(nose)

MP3 005

눈

눈을 감다
close[shut]
one's eyes

눈을 사르르/지그시 감다
close one's eyes
softly/gently

눈을 뜨다
open one's eyes

눈을 치켜뜨다
(지루함, 짜증, 불만을 표현)
roll one's eyes

~를 곁눈으로 보다,
의심의 눈초리로 보다
look askance at ~

~를 노려보다, 흘겨보다
look angrily[sharply] at ~,
glare at ~

시선[눈길]을 돌리다
avert[turn away]
one's eyes,
look away

곁눈질하다, 흘낏 보다
look out of the corner
of one's eyes

SENTENCES TO USE

나는 무서운 장면에서 눈을 감았다.　　　　I closed my eyes during the scary scene.

그가 자기 자랑하는 걸 듣고 그녀는 눈을 치켜떴다.　Hearing him brag about himself, she rolled her eyes.

요즘 많은 이들이 공공 부문에서 일하는 사람들을 의심의 눈초리로 본다.
These days, many people look askance at the people working in the public sector.

그녀는 내 질문에 답하지 않고 나를 노려보기만 했다　She didn't answer my question and just glared at me.

내가 그를 보고 있는 것을 그가 알아채는 바람에 나는 황급히 시선을 돌렸다.
He caught me looking at him, so I quickly averted my eyes.

눈을 깜박이다
blink (one's eyes)

눈을 가늘게 뜨다, 실눈을 뜨다
squint (at ~), narrow one's eyes

눈을 찡긋하다, 윙크하다
wink (at ~)

눈 하나 깜짝 안 하다
not bat an eye

눈을 내리깔다
lower one's eyes,
look down

눈을 비비다
rub one's eyes

눈을 가리다
cover one's eyes

눈을 붙이다
sleep, have a sleep,
take[have] a nap

SENTENCES TO USE

그녀는 눈을 가늘게 뜨고 간판을 쳐다보았다.	She squinted at the sign.
제임스는 나에게 눈을 찡긋하며 지나갔다.	James winked at me as he passed by.
그는 얘기하면서 눈을 자주 깜박였다.	He often blinked as he talked.
그 아이는 눈을 내리깔고 아무 말도 하지 않았다.	The child lowered his eyes and said nothing.
눈을 너무 자주 비비지 마.	Don't rub your eyes too often.

코를 골다
snore

코를[콧물을] 닦다
wipe one's (runny) nose

코를 파다[후비다]
pick one's nose

코를 풀다
blow
one's nose

코를 킁킁하다, 훌쩍이다
sniffle

(화가 나서) 코를 벌름거리다
flare
one's nostrils

코를 긁다
scratch one's
nose

~에 코를 박고 있다
have one's nose in ~
(책이나 잡지, 신문을 집중해서 읽는다는 의미)

큰코다치다
pay dearly
(구식 표현)

SENTENCES TO USE

그녀는 남편이 코를 너무 크게 골아서 함께 잠을 못 잔다.
She can't sleep with her husband because he snores so loudly.

그 아이는 만화책을 보면서 자꾸 코를 후빈다.
The child keeps picking his nose while reading comic books.

그만 훌쩍거리고 코 좀 풀어.　　　　　　Stop sniffling and blow your nose.

사람이 코를 긁으면 거짓말을 하고 있다는 의미라고 한다.
If a person scratches his or her nose, it means he or she is lying.

주말이면 그 소녀는 늘 책에 코를 박고 있다.　　　On weekends, the girl always has her nose in the book.

6 입(mouth), 입술(lip)

MP3 006

입

입을 다물다
shut one's mouth,
close one's mouth

입을 꼭[굳게] 다물다
shut one's
mouth firmly[tight]

손으로 입을 가리다
put one's hand over one's mouth,
cover one's mouth with one's hand

입을 벌리다, 입을 열다
(말하다, 이야기를 꺼내다)
open one's
mouth

입을 크게 벌리다
open one's
mouth wide

입을 닦다
wipe one's
mouth

입을 맞추다
(뽀뽀하다)
kiss

입을 맞추다(말을 맞추다)
get one's story
straight

입을 오물거리다
mumble

SENTENCES TO USE

입 다물고 밥이나 먹어.	Shut your mouth and eat your meal.
그는 입을 굳게 다물고 아무 말도 하지 않았다.	He shut his mouth firmly and said nothing.
눈은 감고 입을 벌려 주세요.	Please close your eyes and open your mouth.
그녀는 휴지로 입을 닦았다.	She wiped her mouth with a tissue.
그녀는 그의 뺨에 가볍게 입을 맞췄다.	She kissed him lightly on his cheek.

입술을 핥다,
입맛을 다시다
lick one's lips

입술을 깨물다
bite one's lip

입술을 오므리다
purse one's lips

입술[입]을 삐죽 내밀다
pout

입술이 떨리다, 입술을 떨다
one's lips quiver

입술에 손가락을 갖다 대다
put[lay] one's finger to one's lips
(입을 다물라는 신호)

입술에 ～를 바르다
apply ~ to one's lips,
put ~ on one's lips

SENTENCES TO USE

맛있는 음식들을 생각하며 그는 입맛을 다셨다.   Thinking of delicious foods, he licked his lips.

그녀는 입술을 깨무는 버릇이 있다.   She has a habit of biting her lip.

그 아이는 엄마가 게임을 못 하게 하자 입술을 삐죽 내밀었다.
The child pouted when his mother prevented him from playing the game.

그 여자는 입술에 손가락을 갖다 대고 "쉿!"이라고 말했다.
The woman put her finger to her lips and said, "Shh!"

입술이 말랐구나. 입술에 립글로스 좀 바르렴.   Your lips are dry. Apply some lip gloss to your lips.

혀(tongue), 치아(tooth)

MP3 007

혀

혀를 깨물다, 하고 싶은 말을 참다
bite one's tongue

(~에게) 혀를 내밀다
stick one's tongue out (at ~)

혀를 날름거리다
stick one's tongue out a lot,
dart one's tongue
in and out

혀를 차다
click one's tongue

혀를 굴리다
roll one's tongue

혀를 놀리다, 지껄이다,
나불거리다
wag one's tongue

(강아지 등이) 혀를 빼물다
have[stick] one's
tongue out

혀를 빼물고
with one's
tongue out

SENTENCES TO USE

나는 밥을 너무 빨리 먹다가 혀를 깨물었다.   I bit my tongue while eating too quickly.

그 아이는 엄마에게 혀를 내밀고는 도망쳤다.
The child stuck his tongue out at his mother and ran away.

우리 엄마는 내 말을 듣고 혀를 찼다.   My mom clicked her tongue when she heard me.

그는 쉬지 않고 혀를 놀렸다.   He kept wagging his tongue.

날이 더워서 그 개는 혀를 빼물고 엎드려 있었다.
Because of the hot weather, the dog was lying on its stomach with its tongue out.

이를 닦다, 양치질을 하다
brush one's teeth

치실질을 하다
floss (one's teeth),
use dental floss

치간칫솔질을 하다
use an interdental
(tooth)brush

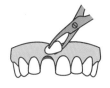

이를 뽑다
have a tooth
removed[pulled (out)]

이를 치료하다
have one's
tooth[teeth]
treated

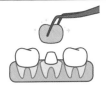

이에 금을 씌우다
have[get] one's tooth[teeth]
crowned with gold

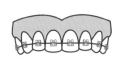

이를 교정하다
have[get] one's
teeth straightened,
wear[have] braces

스케일링을 받다
have one's
teeth scaled

이를 갈다
grind
one's teeth

분해서 이를 갈다
gnash one's
teeth

이를 악물다
clench one's
jaw

**(이쑤시개로)
이를 쑤시다**
pick one's teeth

SENTENCES TO USE

양치질 후에 치실질이나 치간칫솔질도 해야 한다.
You should floss or use an interdental brush after brushing your teeth.

나는 어제 사랑니를 뽑았다.
I had one of my wisdom teeth removed yesterday.

그 아이는 치아 교정을 하는 중이다.
The child is wearing braces.

스케일링을 매년 받는 게 좋다.
You should have your teeth scaled every year.

그 사람은 잘 때 이를 간다.
He grinds his teeth when he sleeps.

통증이 너무 심해서 나는 이를 악물어야 했다.
The pain was so bad that I had to clench my jaw.

귀

~에 귀를 기울이다
listen carefully
to ~

~에 귀를 막다[닫다]
close one's ears
to ~

귀를 파다[후비다]
pick one's ear(s)

귀를 뚫다
have[get]
one's ear(s)
pierced

~의 귀를 잡아당기다
pull
someone's ear

턱

턱을 들다
lift[raise] one's chin,
hold one's chin up high

턱을 내밀다
stick out one's chin

턱을 아래로 당기다
pull one's chin
down

턱을 만지다
touch one's chin

턱을 쓰다듬다
rub one's chin

손으로 턱을 괴다
hold one's chin in one's hand(s),
cup one's chin in one's hands

* chin과 jaw
chin과 jaw는 모두 우리말로
'턱'이라고 하지만 차이가 있다.
jaw는 귀 밑의 얼굴 아래쪽
턱 전체를 가리키고, chin은
jaw의 앞 끝부분을 가리킨다.

SENTENCES TO USE

그 사람은 상사의 불평불만에 귀를 닫았다.　　He closed his ears to his boss's complaints.

그는 사람들 앞에서 자꾸 손가락으로 귀를 후빈다.
He keeps picking his ears with his fingers in front of people.

나는 스무 살 때 귀를 뚫었다.　　I had my ears pierced when I was 20 years old.

그 남자 후보는 토론회에서 말을 할 때마다 턱을 들었다.
The male candidate raised his chin whenever he spoke at the debate.

그녀는 손으로 턱을 괴고 있었다.　　She was holding her chin in her hand.

볼·뺨

볼[얼굴]을 붉히다
turn red, blush

볼을 비비다
rub one's cheek (against someone's)

볼을 쓰다듬다
stroke one's[someone's] cheek

뺨을 부풀리다
puff out one's
cheeks

혀로 한쪽 볼을 부풀리다
put[stick] one's tongue
in one's cheek

뺨을 때리다
slap someone on the cheek[face],
slap someone's cheek[face]

뺨을 꼬집다
pinch someone's cheek,
give someone a pinch on the cheek

SENTENCES TO USE

그 소녀는 칭찬을 듣자 얼굴을 붉혔다.	The girl blushed when she heard the compliment.
그 여성은 아기의 볼에 자기 볼을 비볐다.	The woman rubbed her cheek against the baby's.
나는 고양이의 볼을 쓰다듬었다.	I stroked the cat's cheek.
아이는 심심한 듯 뺨을 부풀리고 있었다.	The child was puffing out his cheeks as if bored.
그 남자는 귀엽다면서 남자아이의 볼을 꼬집었다.	The man pinched the boy's cheek, saying he was cute.

9 목(neck, throat)

MP3 009

목을 돌리다
screw one's head around

목을 주무르다
massage someone's
[one's] neck

목을 뒤로 젖히다
bend[lean] one's
neck back(ward)

목을 풀다
warm up one's voice

목을 가다듬다
clear one's throat

목에 ~이 걸리다
choke on ~

목을 조르다
choke someone

목을 졸라 죽이다
strangle someone,
choke someone to death

목을 매다
hang oneself

SENTENCES TO USE

나는 뒷목이 아파서 주물렀다.
I massaged the back of my neck because it hurt.

그 가수는 노래하기 전에 목을 가다듬었다.
The singer cleared her throat before singing.

잠시 쉬려고 나는 의자에 앉아 목을 뒤로 젖혔다.
To rest for a while, I sat in a chair and leaned my neck back.

범인은 피해자의 목을 졸라 죽였다.
The criminal strangled the victim.

그 사람은 목을 맸으나 죽지 않았다.
The man hanged himself but he didn't die.

10 얼굴 표정(facial expression)

MP3 010

얼굴을 찡그리다
make a face,
frown

미소 짓다
smile

이를 드러내며 웃다
grin

소리 내어 웃다
laugh

킥킥거리다, 키득거리다
giggle

~를 비웃다, 냉소하다
laugh at, mock, ridicule,
sneer at, make fun of

윙크하다
wink

코를 찡그리다
wrinkle one's nose

눈물을 흘리다
weep, cry

흑흑 흐느껴 울다
sob, cry

얼굴을 붉히다
blush, turn red

눈을 치켜뜨다
(지루함, 짜증, 불만을 나타내는 표정)
roll one's eyes

SENTENCES TO USE

그 아이는 약을 보고 얼굴을 찡그렸다.	The child frowned at the medicine.
그 남자는 어린 아들을 보고 이를 드러내고 웃었다.	The man grinned at his little boy.
그는 책을 읽으며 키득거렸다.	He giggled as he read a book.
그녀는 음식물 쓰레기 냄새에 코를 찡그렸다.	She wrinkled her nose when she smelled the food waste.
영화의 그 장면에서 많은 이들이 흐느껴 울었다.	Many people sobbed at that scene in the movie.

CHAPTER

2

상반신

UPPER BODY

어깨(shoulder)

MP3 011

어깨를 으쓱하다
shrug
(one's shoulders)

어깨를 들썩거리다
move one's shoulders
up and down

어깨를 펴다
straighten one's
shoulders

어깨를 움츠리다
hunch one's
shoulders

어깨를 주무르다
massage someone's
shoulders

~의 어깨를 토닥이다
pat someone
on the shoulder

어깨를 감싸 안다
embrace someone's
shoulder

어깨에 ~를 둘러매다
carry ~ on[over]
one's shoulder

어깨 동무를 하다
put arms around
each other's
shoulders

어깨동무를 하고
with one's arms
around each other's
shoulders

어깨를 나란히 하고 서다
stand shoulder to
shoulder

어깨를 나란히 하다 (비유적)
rank with,
be equal to

SENTENCES TO USE

줄리아는 그의 질문에 말없이 어깨를 으쓱했다.
Julia shrugged silently at his question.

그녀는 추워서 어깨를 움츠리고 걸었다.
She walked hunching her shoulders as it was cold.

그 소녀는 자주 할머니의 어깨를 주물러 드린다.
The girl often massages her grandmother's shoulders.

선생님은 그 학생의 어깨를 토닥였다.
The teacher patted the student on the shoulder.

두 아이는 어깨동무를 하고 걸어갔다.
The two children walked with their arms around each other's shoulders.

2 팔(arms), 팔꿈치(elbow)

MP3 012

 팔

(양)팔을 들다
raise one's arm(s)

(양)팔을 내리다
lower one's arm(s)

팔을 벌리다
open one's
arms

팔을 벌리고
with one's arms
open

팔을 뻗다
reach[stretch] out
one's arm(s)

양팔을 앞으로 뻗다
extend one's
arms

팔을 구부리다
bend one's arm(s)

팔을 구부려 알통을 만들다
flex one's arm

팔을 휘두르다
swing one's arms

팔을[소매를] 걷어붙이다
roll[turn] up
one's sleeves

팔을 베고 옆으로 눕다
lie with one's arm
under one's head,
lie using one's arm as a pillow

SENTENCES TO USE

두 팔을 머리 위로 똑바로 드세요.   Raise your arms straight above your head.

아이는 팔을 활짝 벌리고 달려 왔다.   The child came running with his arms open wide.

나는 팔을 뻗어 옷장 선반에서 상자를 내렸다.
I stretched out my arms and lowered the box from the closet shelf.

그는 팔을 구부려 알통을 만들어 근육을 과시했다.   He flexed his arm to show off his muscles.

그는 팔을 걷어붙이고 상자들을 나르기 시작했다.   He rolled up his sleeves and started carrying the boxes.

팔을 잡다
hold[grab] someone's arm,
hold[take, catch, seize]
someone by the arm

팔을 뿌리치다
shake off someone's arm

팔을 잡아끌다
pull someone's arm

팔에 매달리다
cling to someone's arm

팔짱을 끼다 (혼자)
fold one's arms

팔짱을 끼고[낀 채] (혼자)
with one's arms folded

~의 팔을 비틀다
twist someone's arm

팔짱을 끼다 (타인과)
lock one's arms
together

팔짱을 끼고[낀 채] (타인과)
arm in arm (with ~)

SENTENCES TO USE

누군가가 내 팔을 잡으며 내 이름을 불렀다.
Someone grabbed my arm and called my name.

그녀는 팔짱을 낀 채 생각에 잠겨 있었다.
She was lost in thought with her arms folded.

그는 자기 어머니와 팔짱을 끼고 걸어가고 있었다.
He was walking arm in arm with his mother.

팔꿈치를 ~에 올려놓다   팔꿈치를 ~에 올려놓고
put elbows on ~   with elbows on ~

팔꿈치로 찌르다
nudge[jog, jostle] with
one's elbow

팔꿈치로 헤치고 가다
elbow one's way through ~

SENTENCES TO USE

팔꿈치를 식탁에 올려놓고 식사를 하는 건 예의에 어긋난다고 여겨진다.
It is considered rude to eat with your elbows on the table.

그는 팔꿈치로 사람들을 밀치고 지나갔다.
He elbowed his way through the crowd.

3 손목(wrist), 손(hand), 손등(back of one's hand), 손바닥(palm)

MP3 013

손목

손목을 잡다
hold[grab] someone's wrist,
hold[take, grab, catch, seize]
someone by the wrist

손목을 돌리다
turn
one's wrist

손목을 삐다
sprain
one's wrist

손

손을 들다
raise
one's hand

손을 들고
with
one's hand(s) up

손을 내리다
lower
one's hand

(~와) 악수하다
shake hands (with ~)

~의 손을 잡다
hold someone's
hand

(두 사람이) 손을 잡다
hold each
other's hands

손을 잡고
hand in hand

(자신의) 두 손을 깍지 끼다
clasp one's hands

SENTENCES TO USE

그가 내 손목을 잡았을 때 가슴이 뛰었다.

My heart was pounding when he grabbed my wrist.

그는 농구를 하다가 손목을 삐었다.

He sprained his wrist playing basketball.

그 아이는 손을 들고 횡단보도를 건넜다.

The child crossed the crosswalk with his hand up.

시장은 참석자들과 악수했다.

The mayor shook hands with the attendees.

아이는 엄마의 손을 잡고 있다.

The child is holding her mother's hand.

주먹을 쥐다
clench
one's fist(s)

합장하다
put[have] one's hands
together in front of the
chest[as if in prayer]

손을 펴다
open
one's hand

손으로 햇빛을 가리다
shade the sun with
one's hand(s)

~에 손을 넣다
put one's hand in ~

~에서 손을 빼다
take one's hand
out of ~

손을 씻다
wash one's
hands

손을 흔들다
wave one's
hand

~의 손을 움켜쥐다
grasp someone's hand

~의 손을 뿌리치다
shake off
someone's hand

~에게 손을 내밀다
reach[stretch, hold] out
one's hand to ~

SENTENCES TO USE

그는 그 이야기를 듣고 화가 나 주먹을 꽉 쥐었다.   He clenched his fist in anger when he heard the story.

그는 주머니에서 손을 뺐다.   He took his hand out of his pocket.

그 사람들은 활주로로 나아가는 비행기를 향해 손을 흔들었다.
The people waved their hands at the plane going down the runway.

그녀는 그의 손을 뿌리치며 비명을 질렀다.   She shook off his hand and screamed.

앞서 올라가던 사람이 나에게 손을 내밀었다.
The person who was going up ahead reached out his hand to me.

손을 허리에 대다
put one's hands
on one's hips

손을 허리에 대고
with one's hands
on one's hips

손을 떨다,
손이 떨리다
hands
tremble[shake]

손을 비비다
rub one's hands
(together)

손을 호호 불다
blow on
one's hands

손등, 손바닥

불에 손을 쬐다
warm one's hands
by[over] the fire

손등으로 이마의 땀을 닦다
wipe the sweat off one's forehead
with the back of one's hand

손등으로 입을 닦다
wipe one's mouth with
the back of one's hand

손등에 입을 맞추다
kiss someone's hand,
kiss someone on the back
of someone's hand

하이파이브를
하다
highfive

(서로) 손바닥을 맞대다
put our/your/their
palms together

남의 손바닥을 때리다
hit someone
on the palm

SENTENCES TO USE

슈퍼맨이 손을 허리에 대고 서 있다.
Superman is standing with his hands on his hips.

그녀는 너무 긴장해서 손을 떨고 있었다.
She was so nervous that her hands were trembling.

나는 손이 시려서 두 손을 비볐다.
I rubbed my hands together since they were cold.

그는 손등으로 이마의 땀을 닦았다.
He wiped the sweat off his forehead with the back of his hand.

서양에서는 남성이 여성의 손등에 입을 맞추는 것이 드문 일이 아니었다.
In the West, it was not uncommon for men to kiss women on the back of their hands.

UNIT 4 손가락(finger), 손톱(fingernail)

MP3 014

손가락

손가락을 쫙 펴다
spread one's fingers

손가락을 접다
fold one's fingers

손가락으로 ~를 가리키다,
~를 손가락질하다
point ~, point one's finger at ~

손가락으로 ~를 만지다
feel ~ with one's fingers

손가락으로 ~의 수를 세다
count ~ on[with] one's fingers

엄지척을 하다
give a thumbs-up

손가락에 반지를 끼다
put a ring on one's finger(동작)
wear[have] a ring on one's finger(상태)

손가락에서 반지를 빼다
take one's ring off

SENTENCES TO USE

손가락을 쫙 펴 보세요. 약지가 검지보다 길군요.
Spread your fingers. Your ring finger is longer than your index finger.

손가락으로 달을 가리키는데 손가락만 보지 마라.
When I point my finger at the moon, don't look only at my finger.

사람을 손가락질하는 건 예의에 어긋난 행동이다.   It's not polite to point your finger at people.

감독이 선수에게 엄지척을 해 보였다.   The coach gave a thumbs-up to the player.

손가락 마디를 꺾어서
소리를 내다
crack one's
fingers[knuckles]

손가락을 빨다
suck one's finger,
live from hand to mouth
(간신히 먹고 살다)

손가락을 베이다
cut one's
finger

손가락 하나
까딱하지 않다
not lift a finger,
not do anything

손톱

손톱을 (짧게) 깎다
cut[clip] one's
(finger)nails (short)

손톱을 다듬다
trim one's
(finger)nails

(긴장해서) 손톱을 물어뜯다
bite one's
(finger)nails

손톱으로 긁다[할퀴다]
scratch with
one's (finger)nails

네일을 받다
get one's nails done, get a manicure
손톱에 매니큐어를 칠하다
manicure one's nails, apply nail polish

손톱이 부러지다
break one's
(finger)nail

손톱이 빠지다
lose one's (finger)nail,
one's (finger)nail falls
off[falls out]

SENTENCES TO USE

손가락 마디를 꺾어서 소리를 내는 게 안 좋나요?	Is cracking your knuckles bad for them?
종이에 손가락을 베였어요.	I cut my finger on a piece of paper.
손톱을 너무 짧게 깎지 마세요.	Don't cut your nails too short.
그는 손톱을 물어뜯는 오랜 버릇을 최근에 버렸어요.	He recently gave up his old habit of biting his nails.
애니는 매주 네일숍에서 네일을 받는다.	Annie gets her nails done at the nail salon every week.

5 등/허리(back), 허리(waist), 배(abdomen, belly)

MP3 015

등/허리

등을[허리를] 펴다
straighten one's back,
straighten[stretch]
oneself

허리를[몸을] 굽히다
bend forward,
bend down

허리를 굽실거리다,
아부하다
kiss someone's ass

~에 등을 기대다
lean back
against ~

허리[상체]를 뒤로 젖히다
lean back

~에게 등을 돌리다
turn one's back on[to] ~

등(짝)을 후려치다
slap a person
on the back

등을 토닥거리다
pat someone
on the back

등을 떠밀다
push someone's
back

등에 ~를 업다
carry ~ on one's
back

SENTENCES TO USE

허리를 펴고 앞을 보세요.
Straighten your back and look forward.

척추에 압박을 가하지 않고 몸을 굽히는 법을 익혀야 해요.
You should learn to bend forward without putting pressure on your spine.

그녀는 소파에 등을 기대고 앉아서 책을 읽고 있다.　She is reading a book leaning back against the sofa.

그 사건 후로 대부분의 사람들이 그에게서 등을 돌렸다.
Most people turned their backs on him after the incident.

옛날에는 엄마들이 아기를 등에 업는 경우가 많았다.
In the past, mothers often carried their baby on their back.

허리가 아프다
one's back hurts,
have back pain

등을 긁다
scratch one's back

등에 청진기를 대다
put a stethoscope
on one's back

허리

허리를 다치다
hurt one's back[waist]

허리를 삐다
put one's back out

허리를 비틀다
twist one's waist

허리띠를 하다
wear a[one's] belt

허리띠를 졸라매다, 절약하다
tighten a[one's] belt,
draw a belt tighter

'허리'를 뜻하는 단어들
- **back** : 등, 등에서 내려오는 뒤쪽 허리.
- **waist** : 허리의 잘록한 부분.

SENTENCES TO USE

책상에 너무 오래 앉아 있었더니 허리가 아프다.
My back hurts from sitting at the desk for too long.

그는 자로 등을 긁었다.
He scratched his back with a ruler.

의사가 숨소리를 듣기 위해 환자의 등에 청진기를 댔다.
The doctor put a stethoscope on the patient's back to hear her breathing.

그 사람은 신발을 신다가 허리를 삐었다.
The man put his back out when he was putting on his shoes.

우리는 수입이 줄어서 허리띠를 졸라매야 했다.
We had to tighten our belts because we were making less money.

배

배가 고프다
be hungry

배가 부르다
be full

배가 아프다
have a stomachache

GrOOOWl...

배에서 꼬르륵 소리가 나다
one's stomach is growling

배를 내밀다
stick out one's belly

배를 내밀고, 불룩한 배로
with one's belly sticking out

배를 깔고 눕다, 엎드리다
lie on one's stomach

엎드려서
on one's stomach

배를 문지르다
rub one's belly[stomach]

배가 나오다
have[get] a potbelly

배가 들어가다, 뱃살이 빠지다
lose belly fat

'배'를 뜻하는 단어들
- **stomach :** 배를 가리키는 일반적인 말로, '위장'과 관련 있을 때 주로 사용.
- **belly :** '배'라는 신체 부위를 가리키는 말.
- **abdomen :** '복부'를 뜻하는 전문 용어.

SENTENCES TO USE

배가 너무 고파서 뭐든지 먹을 수 있을 것 같아요.　　I'm so hungry I could eat a horse.

그 여자는 배를 내밀고 걷는다.　　The woman walks with her belly sticking out.

엎드려서 책을 읽는 건 허리에 안 좋아요.　　Reading a book on your stomach is bad for your back.

강아지들은 사람들이 배 만져 주는 걸 좋아한다.　　Puppies like people to rub their belly.

40이 되면서 배가 나왔어요.　　I've had a potbelly since I turned 40.

CHAPTER

3

하반신

LOWER BODY

엉덩이(hip, butt), 골반(pelvis)

MP3 016

엉덩이

엉덩이를 실룩거리다
sway one's hips

엉덩이를 들썩거리다
move one's hips
up and down

엉덩이를 흔들다
shake[rock, swing] one's hips

엉덩이를 (자리에서) 떼다, 들다
lift one's hips

엉덩이를 뒤로 빼다
move the hips back

엉덩이를 토닥거리다
pat someone
on the hip

엉덩이를 긁다
scratch one's butt

엉덩이를 찰싹 때리다
slap one's butt, slap
someone on someone's butt

엉덩이의 먼지를 털다
dust off the
bottom of one's pants

엉덩이를 까다 (바지를 내리다)
take down
one's pants

골반

골반을 흔들다
shake[move]
one's pelvis

바지/치마를 골반에 걸치다
wear one's pants/skirt
over one's pelvis

hip과 butt
우리말로는 둘 다 '엉덩이'라고 하지만 실제로는
차이가 있다.
- **hip :** 허리와 다리가 만나는 골반 부위.
- **butt(buttocks) :** 뒤에서 바라볼 때 보이는
  둥그렇게 튀어나온 부위.
그 외에 behind나 backside, bottom도 '엉덩이'
라는 뜻으로 쓰인다.

SENTENCES TO USE

무용수가 음악에 맞춰 엉덩이를 흔들고 있다.
The dancer is shaking his hips to the music.

그 남자 배우는 엉덩이를 실룩거리며 걷는다.
The actor walks with his hips swaying.

엄마가 아기의 엉덩이를 토닥거렸다.
The mother patted the baby on the hip.

친구가 내 엉덩이를 찰싹 때렸다.
A friend of mine slapped me on my butt.

그 춤을 출 때는 골반을 많이 흔들어야 한다.
When performing that dance, you have to move your pelvis a lot.

2 다리(leg), 허벅지(thigh)

MP3 **0 1 7**

다리

다리를 꼬다
cross one's legs

다리를 꼬고 앉다
sit with one's legs crossed

책상다리를 하고 앉다
sit cross-legged

다리를 떨다
shake one's leg

다리를 뻗다[쭉 펴다]
stretch[straighten]
one's legs

다리를 쭉 펴고
with one's legs
straight

다리를 벌리다
spread
one's legs

다리를 벌리고 앉다
sit with
one's legs apart

다리를 오므리다
close one's legs

다리를 구부리다
bend one's legs

다리를 주무르다
massage one's legs

다리를 긁다
scratch one's leg

SENTENCES TO USE

다리를 꼬고 앉는 건 골반에 안 좋다.
Sitting with your legs crossed is bad for your hips.

다리를 쭉 펴고 앉아서 상체를 다리 위로 구부리세요.
Sit with your legs straight and bend your upper body over your legs.

지하철에서 다리를 벌리고 앉는 사람들이 있다.
There are people who sit with their legs apart on the subway.

다리를 오므려서 자리를 좀 만들어 봐.
Close your legs and make some room.

그 소녀는 할머니의 다리를 주물러 드렸다.
The girl massaged her grandmother's legs.

한 다리로 서다
stand on one leg

다리를 끌다
drag one's leg

(오른쪽/왼쪽) 다리를 절다
limp (in the right/left leg),
walk with a limp (on[in] the[one's] right/left leg)

다리가 저리다
have pins and needles in one's leg,
one's leg is numb,
have no feelings in one's leg,
one's leg falls asleep

다리에 쥐가 나다
have[get] a cramp
in the leg,
get[be] cramped in the leg

다리를 다치다
hurt[injure]
one's leg

다리가 부러지다
break
one's leg

다리를 절단하다
have one's leg
amputated

다리에 깁스를 하다
wear a cast on
one's leg

**~의 다리를
걸어 넘어뜨리다**
trip someone (up)

SENTENCES TO USE

한 다리로 얼마 동안이나 서 있을 수 있어요?　　　How long can you stand on one leg?

그 사람은 허리 수술을 받은 후로 오른쪽 다리를 살짝 전다.
He walks with a slight limp on his right leg since his back surgery.

오랫동안 책상다리를 하고 앉아 있었더니 다리가 저리다.
After sitting cross-legged for a long time, my legs are numb.

그는 축구를 하다가 다리를 다쳤다.　　　He hurt his leg while playing soccer.

그 남자는 다리에 깁스를 하고 있다.　　　The man is wearing a cast on his leg.

(남의) 허벅지를 쓰다듬다
stroke someone's thigh

(남의) 허벅지를 때리다
slap[hit] someone's thigh,
slap[hit] someone on the thigh

(자신의) 허벅지를 꼬집다
pinch one's thigh
(꿈인지 생시인지 믿기지 않아) 허벅지를 꼬집어 보다
pinch oneself to see if one is dreaming

SENTENCES TO USE

그녀는 큰소리로 웃으면서 옆에 앉은 친구의 허벅지를 때렸다.
She laughed out loud and slapped her friend next to her on the thigh.

나는 시험 공부를 해야 했지만 몹시 졸렸다. 그래서 허벅지를 꼬집었다.
I had to study for the exam, but I was very sleepy, so I pinched my thigh.

무릎

무릎을 구부리다	무릎을 세우다	무릎을 세우고	무릎을 끌어안다	한쪽 무릎을 꿇다
bend one's knees	draw up one's knees	with one's knees up	hug one's knees, put one's arms around one's knees	go down on one knee

무릎을 꿇다	무릎을 꿇고	~와 무릎을 맞대다	무릎을 맞대고	무릎걸음으로 가다
kneel down, go[fall] down on one's knees, drop to[on] one's knees	on one's knees	get knee to knee with ~	knee to knee	go on one's knees

무릎을 치다, 때리다
slap[hit] someone's lap

~의 무릎을 베다
lie on someone's lap, lay[rest] one's head on[in] someone's lap

무릎이 까지다
have[get] one's knee(s) skinned[scraped], scrape one's knee(s)

knee와 lap
둘 다 우리말로는 '무릎'이지만 차이가 있다.
• knee : 다리가 접히는 부분
• lap : 자리에 앉았을 때 두 다리 위의 넓적한 부분

SENTENCES TO USE

그 자세를 할 때는 무릎을 90도로 구부려야 해요.
You have to bend your knees 90 degrees when you do that position.

그녀는 무릎을 끌어안고 바닥에 앉아 있었다.　　She was sitting on the floor hugging her knees.

그는 무릎을 꿇고 바닥에서 종이를 집었다.　　He knelt down to pick up the paper from the floor.

나는 아직 신을 신은 채였기 때문에 무릎걸음으로 방에 들어갔다.
I entered the room on my knees because I still had my shoes on.

그는 잔디밭에서 여자 친구의 무릎을 베고 누워 있었다.
He was lying on his girlfriend's lap on the lawn.

종아리

종아리를 마사지하다
massage one's calves

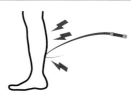

종아리를 때리다
hit[whip, lash] someone's calves

종아리를 맞다
get hit[whipped, lashed] on the calves

정강이

~의 정강이를 차다
kick someone in the shin

~에 정강이를 부딪치다
bump[hit] one's shin against ~

calf와 shin
- **calf(종아리)** : 아래 다리(무릎과 발목 사이)의 뒤쪽 부분
- **shin(정강이)** : 아래 다리(무릎과 발목 사이)의 앞쪽 뼈가 있는 부분

정강이가 까지다
have[get] one's shin scraped[skinned]

SENTENCES TO USE

달리기를 하고 나서 나는 종아리를 마사지했다.　　After running, I massaged my calves.

나는 어렸을 때 잘못을 하면 부모님께 종아리를 맞았다.
When I was a child, I got whipped on the calves by my parents if I did something wrong.

그 사람은 자기 부하 직원의 정강이를 발로 찼다.　　He kicked his subordinate in the shin.

나는 침대 모서리에 정강이를 부딪쳤다.　　I bumped my shin against the corner of the bed.

그는 축구를 하다가 정강이가 까졌다.　　He got his shin scraped while playing soccer.

4 발(foot), 발목(ankle), 발바닥(sole of one's foot), 발꿈치(heel)

MP3 **019**

발

발을 헛디디다
trip, stumble, lose[miss] one's footing

~에 발이 걸려 넘어지다
trip over

발을 질질 끌다
drag one's foot[feet]

발을 마사지하다
massage one's foot[feet]

발 스트레칭을 하다
stretch one's foot[feet]

발을 구르다
stomp one's foot[feet]

발을 내딛다
set foot, take a step (forward)

발을 멈추다
stop

발(길)을 돌리다
turn back, turn away, turn[direct] one's steps (toward ~)

~를 발로 차다
kick ~

~를 발로 밟다
step on ~

~와 발을 맞추다
keep pace with ~, fall into step with ~

족욕을 하다
soak one's feet
(in warm water)

SENTENCES TO USE

그는 계단에서 발을 헛디뎌서 굴러 떨어졌다.
He tripped on the stairs and tumbled all the way down.

그 영화에서 범인은 발을 질질 끌며 걸었다. In the movie, the criminal dragged his feet.

도서관이 휴관이어서 우리는 발길을 돌려야 했다. The library was closed, so we had to turn away.

하이힐을 신은 여성이 지하철에서 내 발을 밟았다.
A woman in high heels stepped on my foot on the subway.

~계에 발을 들여 놓다
(~ 분야에서 일을 시작하다)
take the[one's] first step into ~,
start work in ~

~에서 발을 빼다 (관계를 끊다)
wash one's hands of ~,
back out of ~,
sever connections[relations] with ~

~에 발을 끊다
stop visiting ~,
keep away from ~

발목

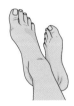

발목을 교차하다
cross one's ankles

발목을 삐다[접질리다]
sprain one's ankle

발목을 돌리다
turn one's ankle

발목을 펴다
stretch one's ankle

발목을 몸쪽으로 당기다
pull one's ankle
toward one's body

~에 발목 잡히다
be tied to ~,
be chained to ~,
be pressed with ~

(발목에) 전자발찌를 차다
wear an electronic
monitoring anklet

SENTENCES TO USE

그는 그 밴드의 베이시스트로 음악계에 첫발을 내디뎠다.
He took his first step into the music scene as the bassist for that band.

나는 이제 전체 상황에서 발을 빼고 싶다.　　　I want to wash my hands of the whole situation.

그녀는 발목을 교차한 채 의자에 앉아 있었다.　　She was sitting on a chair with her ankles crossed.

나는 발이 피로해서 발 마사지를 하고 발목을 돌렸다.
My feet were tired, so I massaged my feet and turned my ankles.

발목을 폈다가 몸 쪽으로 당기세요.　　　　　　Stretch your ankles and pull them toward your body.

발바닥

발바닥을 간질이다	발바닥을 긁다	발바닥에 물집이 잡히다	발바닥에 굳은살이 박이다
tickle the sole of someone's foot	scratch the sole of one's foot	have a blister on the sole of one's foot	have a callus on the sole of one's foot

발꿈치

발꿈치를 들다
lift one's heel(s)

발꿈치를 들고 걷다, 발끝으로 걷다
walk on tiptoes

SENTENCES TO USE

내가 그의 발바닥을 간질였지만 그는 꿈쩍도 하지 않았다.
I tickled the soles of his feet, but he didn't budge.

오늘 하루 종일 새 구두를 신고 다녔더니 발바닥에 물집이 잡혔다.
I've been wearing new shoes all day today, and I've got blisters on the soles of my feet.

그 무용수는 발바닥을 비롯한 발 전체에 굳은살이 박였다.
The dancer has calluses all over her feet, including the soles.

아기가 깰까 봐 우리는 발꿈치를 들고 걸었다.　　　We walked on tiptoes in case the baby woke up.

MP3 020

발가락

발가락을 꼼지락거리다
wiggle[wriggle]
one's toes

발가락을 짝 펴다
spread[stretch]
one's toes

발가락을 구부리다
bend[curl] one's toes

발가락을 주무르다
massage one's toes

발톱

발가락을 쥐다
grasp one's toes

발가락을 깨물다
bite one's toes

발톱을 깎다
clip[cut] one's
toenails

발톱을 다듬다
trim one's
toenails

발톱을 칠하다
paint one's toenails

발톱이 빠지다
one's toenail falls off,
have one's toenail
fall off

발톱을 숨기다
(비유적 표현)
keep one's cards
close to one's vest

발톱을 세우다
(비유적 표현)
sharpen one's
claws

SENTENCES TO USE

아이는 발가락을 꼼지락거리며 TV를 보고 있었다.
The child was watching TV, wiggling his toes.

그녀는 발가락을 짝 펴고 발톱을 칠하고 있었다.
She was spreading her toes and painting her toenails.

아기는 자기 발가락을 깨물고 있었다.
The baby was biting his toes.

나는 3주에 한 번 정도 발톱을 깎는 것 같아.
I think I cut my toenails about once every three weeks.

예전에 발톱 하나가 빠져서 고생을 했다.
Once I had a hard time because one of my toenails fell off.

CHAPTER

4

전신

WHOLE BODY

움직임과 자세

MP3 021

눕다
lie down, lay
oneself down

반듯이 눕다
lie down on
one's back,
lie face up

모로 눕다
lie on one's
side, lie down
sideways

엎드리다
lie on one's
stomach,
lie face down

**몸을
웅크리고 눕다**
lie curled up

**잠을 못 자고
뒤척이다**
toss and
turn

잠에서 깨다, 일어나다
get up, wake up,
get out of bed

**침대에서
벌떡 일어나다**
spring[jump]
out of bed

자리에서 일어나다
stand up, get up,
rise (from ~)

벌떡 일어나다
spring[jump] to
one's feet,
stand up suddenly

똑바로 서다
stand (up) straight,
stand upright

까치발로 서다
(발끝으로 서다)
stand on tiptoes

한 발로 서다
stand on one leg

한 발로 균형을 잡다
balance oneself
on one leg

SENTENCES TO USE

그는 옆으로 누워 자고 있었다.　　　　　He was sleeping lying on his side.

그 아이는 소파에 엎드려 있었다.　　　　The child was lying face down on the couch.

강아지가 몸을 웅크리고 누워 있다.　　　The puppy is lying curled up.

그는 한참을 뒤척이다 잠들었다.
He tossed and turned for a long time before falling asleep.

그녀는 벨소리를 듣고 벌떡 일어났다.　　She jumped to her feet when she heard the bell.

한 발로 서서 얼마나 있을 수 있어요?　　How long can you stand on one leg?

몸을 (왼쪽/오른쪽으로)
돌리다[틀다]
turn[twist] one's
body (to the left/right)

몸을 앞으로
숙이다
lean forward

몸을 왼쪽/오른쪽으로
기울이다
lean one's body to
the left/right

몸을 앞으로 굽히다
bend forward

몸을 뒤로 젖히다
bend back(wards)

책상으로/탁자로
몸을 굽히다
bend over the
[one's] desk/table

책상에 엎드리다
sit in the chair and have
one's head on the desk

몸을 뒤로 기울이다
lean back

의자에 등을 기대고 앉다
sit back
in the chair

자세를 바로 하다
straighten (up)
one's posture

몸을 흔들다
shake[move]
one's body

몸을 꼼지락거리다,
안절부절못하다
fidget

SENTENCES TO USE

몸을 오른쪽으로 돌리고 왼쪽 팔을 드세요.

Turn your body to the right and raise your left arm.

그녀는 몸을 앞으로 숙여서 바위에 적힌 글귀를 읽었다.
She leaned forward and read the words on the rock.

그는 몸을 뒤로 젖히고 하늘을 올려다보았다.

He bent back and looked up at the sky.

그는 의자에 등을 기대고 낮잠을 잤다.

He sat back in the chair and took a nap.

자세를 바로 하도록 늘 신경 써라.

Always take care to straighten your posture.

쭈그리고 앉다
crouch down

몸을 움츠리다
hunch one's body

몸을 낮추다
lower one's body,
lower oneself down

몸을 옹송그리다, 웅크리다
(등을 둥글게 하고 팔다리를 몸에
가까이 붙인 자세)
curl up

(~로) 몸을 떨다
tremble, shudder,
shake oneself (with ~)

비틀거리다
stagger, stumble

몸을 가누다,
균형을 유지하다
keep one's balance

운동하다
work out, exercise

몸을 풀다, 준비운동을 하다
warm up,
do warm-up exercises

SENTENCES TO USE

그는 우체통 뒤에 쭈그리고 앉아 숨었다.　　　He crouched down behind a post box and hid.

그 여자는 어느 추운 겨울밤에 담요를 덮고 몸을 옹송그렸다.
The woman curled up under the blanket on a cold winter's night.

그 남자는 술을 많이 마셔서 비틀거렸다.　　　The man staggered because he drank a lot.

규칙적으로 적당히 운동을 하는 것이 건강에 좋다.
It is good for your health to exercise regularly and moderately.

달리기 전에 준비운동을 해야 한다.　　　You should warm up before going for a run.

2 몸 관리

MP3 022

몸을 청결하게 유지하다
keep oneself
[one's body] clean

샤워하다
shower,
take[have] a shower

더운물로/찬물로 샤워하다
take a hot/cold
shower

몸에 바디워시를[샤워젤을]/
비누를 문지르다
rub body wash[shower gel]/
soap all over one's body

목욕하다
take a bath

더운물로/찬물로 목욕하다
take a hot/
cold bath

탕에 몸을 담그다
soak in a[the] bath

반신욕을 하다
take a lower-body bath,
soak one's lower body in warm water

몸을 녹이다
warm oneself up,
get warm

SENTENCES TO USE

몸을 항상 청결하게 유지하는 게 좋다.
It's good to keep yourself clean all the time.

나는 여름에도 찬물로 샤워를 못 해요.
I can't take a cold shower even in summer.

이제 집에 가서 뜨거운 물로 목욕을 할 거예요.
Now I'll go home and take a hot bath.

일이 많은 날은 뜨거운 탕에 몸을 담그면 스트레스가 풀려요.
On days when I have a lot of work, soaking in a hot bath helps to relieve stress.

한국에서는 많은 사람들이 반신욕을 한다.
In Korea, many people take a lower-body bath.

몸을 따뜻이 하다
keep oneself warm

담요로 몸을 감싸다
wrap oneself in a blanket

소파에 몸을 파묻다
nestle down into
the sofa[couch]

몸을 편하게 하다, 긴장을 풀다
relax one's body

건강을 잃다/해치다
lose/harm[ruin] one's health

회복하다
get well, get better, recover

몸조심하다, 자기 몸을 돌보다
take care of oneself

SENTENCES TO USE

몸을 늘 따뜻하게 하도록 하세요.
Please try to keep yourself warm all the time.

그녀는 소파에 몸을 파묻고 책을 읽고 있다.
She is reading a book nestling down into the sofa.

잠을 충분히 자지 않으면 건강을 해칠 수도 있어요.
If you don't get enough sleep, it could harm your health.

그는 뇌수술을 받았고, 지금 회복하고 있다.
He had brain surgery and is now recovering.

혼자 사는 사람은 항상 자기 몸을 돌봐야 한다.
People who live alone should always take care of themselves.

3 기타

MP3 023

꾸미다, 몸을 치장하다
adorn oneself

옷을 차려입다
get dressed up

거울에 몸을 비춰 보다
look at oneself in the mirror

몸을 숨기다
hide[conceal] oneself

~의 몸을 밀치다
push someone's body

몸을 수색하다
search someone's body

SENTENCES TO USE

그는 옷을 차려입고 데이트를 하러 갔다.   He got dressed up and went on a date.

그녀는 새 옷을 입고 거울에 자기 모습을 비춰 보았다.
She put on her new clothes and looked at herself in the mirror.

그 사람은 속세로부터 몸을 숨겼다.   The man hid himself from the world.

경찰이 용의자의 몸을 수색했다.   The police searched the suspect's body.

PART II

일상생활 속

행동 표현

의

CLOTHING

옷 입기

MP3 **024**

*put on ~과
wear ~ 다음에는
목적어가 와야 하지만
get dressed는 목적어가 필요 없다.
get dressed 자체로
'옷을 입다'라는 뜻이다.

~(옷)을 입다
put on ~(동작),
get dressed(동작),
wear ~(상태)

~(옷)을 벗다
take off ~

~에 머리를 넣다
put one's head in ~

소매에 팔을 넣다
put one's arm in the sleeve

~의 단추를 채우다
button (up) ~

~의 단추를 풀다
unbutton ~

바지의 지퍼를 올리다
zip up one's
fly[pants, trousers]

~의 지퍼를 올리다
zip up ~

지퍼를 내리다
unzip ~

허리띠를 채우다
buckle
one's belt

허리띠를 풀다
unbuckle
one's belt

SENTENCES TO USE

그는 외출하기 위해 옷을 입고 있다.　　　He is getting dressed to go out.

그녀는 집에 돌아와서 재킷을 벗고 소파에 누웠다.
When she got home, she took off her jacket and lay down on the couch.

아이는 티셔츠 소매에 팔을 넣느라 고생하고 있다.
The child is struggling to put his arm in the sleeve of the T-shirt.

오른손을 다쳐서 셔츠의 단추를 잠그기가 힘들다.　　I hurt my right hand, so it's hard to button my shirt.

그는 화장실에 다녀와서 바지 지퍼 올리는 걸 깜빡했다.
He forgot to zip up his pants after going to the bathroom.

소매를 걷다
roll[pull, turn] up
the sleeve

바짓단을 접다
roll[pull, turn]
up one's[the]
pants[trousers]

옷깃을 세우다
turn up
the collar

모자를
쓰다

(동작)
put on
a hat[cap]

(상태)
wear
a hat[cap]

모자를 벗다
take off one's
hat[cap]

모자를 거꾸로
쓰고 있다
wear a cap
backwards

모자를 푹
눌러 쓰고 있다
wear a hat[cap] low
over one's eyes

목에 스카프를 두르다
wear[wrap] a scarf
around one's neck

넥타이를 매다
tie[wear]
a tie[necktie]

넥타이를 풀다
untie[take off]
a tie[necktie]

넥타이를 고쳐 매다
straighten one's
tie[necktie]

셔츠의
커프스단추를 채우다
put on cufflinks

SENTENCES TO USE

그는 날씨가 더워서 셔츠의 소매를 걷었다.
The weather was hot, so he rolled up the sleeves of his shirt.

그 아이는 바지가 너무 길어서 바짓단을 접었다.
The child rolled up his pants because they were too long.

바람이 세게 불어서 그녀는 트렌치코트의 옷깃을 세웠다.
The wind was blowing hard, so she turned up the collar of her trench coat.

그는 모자를 벗고 선생님께 고개 숙여 인사했다.   He took off his hat and bowed to the teacher.

범인은 모자를 푹 눌러 쓰고 있어서 우리는 그의 얼굴을 알아볼 수 없었다.
The criminal was wearing a hat low over his eyes, so we couldn't make out his face.

장갑을 끼다

(동작)
put on (one's)
gloves

(상태)
wear
gloves

장갑을 벗다
take off (one's)
gloves

신발을 신다

(동작)
put on (one's)
shoes

(상태)
wear (one's)
shoes

신발을 벗다
take off (one's)
shoes

귀걸이/목걸이/팔찌/반지를 하다

(동작)
put on earrings/
a necklace/a bracelet/a ring

(상태)
wear earrings/a necklace/
a bracelet/a ring

~(옷)을 어깨에 걸치다
wrap ~ around one's
shoulders

옷을 껴입다
dress in layers,
bundle up

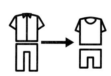

옷을 갈아입다
change (one's)
clothes

입을 옷을/정장을/셔츠를 … 고르다
pick out[choose] clothes/
a suit/a shirt … to wear

SENTENCES TO USE

한국에서는 집에 들어갈 때 신발을 벗어야 한다.
In Korea, you have to take off your shoes when you go inside a house.

그녀는 새로 산 진주 귀걸이를 했다.   She put on her new pearl earrings.

그는 어깨에 스웨터를 걸쳤다.   He wrapped a sweater around his shoulders.

추워서 나는 오늘 옷을 껴입었다.   I bundled up today because it was cold.

그는 땀을 많이 흘려서 옷을 갈아입었다.   He had sweat a lot, so he changed his clothes.

MP3 **025**

빨래하다, 세탁하다
wash (one's) clothes,
do the laundry

세탁기를 돌리다
do the laundry using
the washing machine

~를 손빨래하다
hand-wash ~,
wash ~ by hand

세탁물을 분류하다
sort the laundry

흰 빨랫감과 색깔 있는
빨랫감을 분리하다
separate the colors
from the whites

세탁기에 빨래를 넣다
load the washing machine,
put the laundry in the
washing machine

세제를/섬유유연제를
넣다
add detergent/
fabric softener

빨래를 헹구다
rinse
the laundry

빨래를 탈수하다
spin-dry the
laundry

세탁기에서 빨래를 꺼내다
unload the washing machine,
take the laundry out of the
washing machine

(세탁기에서 꺼낸) 옷을 털다
shake out
the laundry

(건조대에/빨랫줄에)
빨래를 널다
hang (out) the laundry
(on a clothes drying rack/clothesline)

SENTENCES TO USE

오늘 빨래해야 해요.
I have to do the laundry today.

나는 속옷은 손빨래한다.
I hand-wash my underwear.

세탁기에 빨래를 넣은 다음 세제를 넣으세요.
Put the laundry in the washing machine and then add detergent.

섬유유연제를 꼭 넣어야 할까요?
Do I have to add fabric softener?

세탁기에서 빨래를 꺼내서 널어 말려 주세요.
Take the laundry out of the washing machine and hang it out to dry.

빨래를 걷다
get the laundry,
take the laundry off the clothes drying
rack[clothesline]

빨래를 건조기에 넣다
put the laundry in the dryer

빨래를 건조기에서 꺼내다
take the laundry out of the dryer

빨래를 말리다
dry the laundry

빨래를 개다
fold the laundry

빨래를 삶다
boil clothes
[the laundry]

~(옷)에 풀을 먹이다
starch ~

~(옷)을 다림질하다
iron ~

~(옷)에 물을 뿌리다
spray water on ~

~(옷)을 (옷장에) 걸다
hang up ~

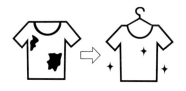

~(옷)을 표백하다
bleach ~

~(옷)을 드라이클리닝 맡기다
have ~ dry cleaned

SENTENCES TO USE

빨래를 건조기에서 꺼냈으면 개야죠.
After you take the laundry out of the dryer, you have to fold it.

오늘 셔츠 5개를 다림질해야 해요.   I need to iron five shirts today.

다림질하기 전에 옷에 물을 뿌려야 해요.
You have to spray water on your clothes before ironing them.

다림질한 셔츠를 옷장에 걸어 주세요.   Please hang up your ironed shirt in the closet.

흰색 셔츠는 가끔 표백해야 한다.   White shirts should be bleached occasionally.

오늘 코트와 재킷을 포함하여 많은 옷을 드라이클리닝 맡겼다.
I dropped off a bunch of clothes, including a coat and a jacket, to have them dry cleaned today.

3 옷 수선, 바느질, 옷 만들기

MP3 **026**

바지/치마/소매 길이를 줄이다

옷을 수선하다
alter[mend]
clothes

(직접)
shorten one's pants/
one's skirt/the sleeves

(남에게 의뢰)
have one's pants/one's skirt/
the sleeves shortened

~(옷)의 품을 줄이다

(직접)
make ~ tighter around
the chest[waist]

(남에게 의뢰)
have ~ made tighter
around the chest[waist]

바느질하다,
꿰매다
sew, stitch

바늘귀에
실을 끼우다
thread a needle

양말의 구멍을 꿰매다
darn one's socks

옷을 직접 만들다
make one's own
clothes, make
clothes oneself

재봉틀을 사용하다
use a sewing
machine

재봉틀로 ~를 박다
sew ~ on a sewing
machine

SENTENCES TO USE

나는 의류 수선집에서 치맛단을 줄였다.	I had my skirt shortened at an alterations shop.
그 사람은 바느질할 줄을 모른다.	He doesn't know how to sew.
나는 양말에 난 구멍을 꿰매서 다시 신었다.	I darned my socks and wore them again.
그 여성은 가끔 옷을 직접 만들어 입는다.	The woman sometimes makes her own clothes.
그녀는 재봉틀을 써서 쿠션을 만들었다.	She made a cushion using a sewing machine.

4 셀프 빨래방 이용법

MP3 027

동전을 준비하다
have one's
coins ready

지폐를 동전으로 교환하다
get change

세제와 섬유 유연제
시트를 구입하다
buy detergent and
fabric softener sheets

세탁기를 선택하다
choose a machine

세탁물을 투입하다
put the laundry
in the washing
machine

세제를 넣다
add detergent

세탁기 문을 닫고
손잡이를 돌려 밀폐하다
close the door and
turn the handle to seal it

세탁 코스를 선택하다
choose a
laundry cycle

동전을 넣다
insert coins

세탁물을 꺼내다
take the laundry
out of the machine

세탁물을 건조기에 넣다
put the laundry
in the dryer

섬유 유연제 시트를 넣다
add fabric softener
sheets

Dry normal,
low heat

Dry normal,
medium heat

Dry normal,
high heat

건조 온도를 설정하다
set the
drying temperature

동전을 넣다
insert coins

시작 버튼을 누르다
press the
START button

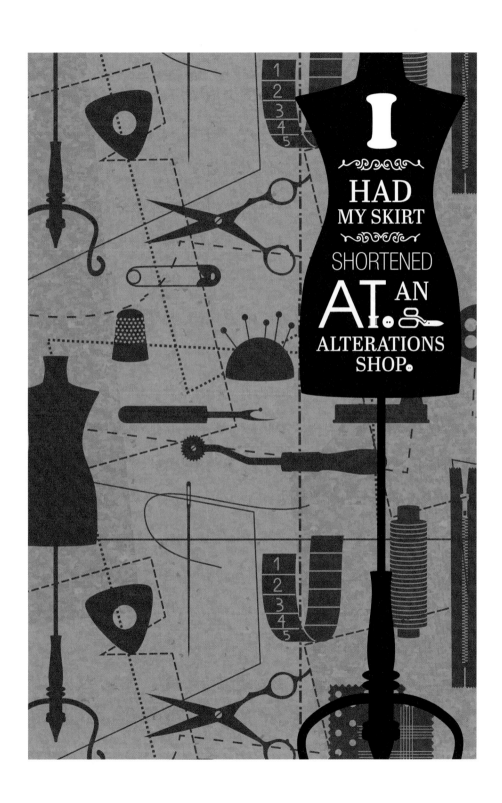

I HAD MY SKIRT SHORTENED AT AN ALTERATIONS SHOP.

CHAPTER

2

식

FOOD

식재료 손질, 보관

MP3 028

~를 찬장에 넣다
put ~ in the
cupboard

~를 냉장고[냉장실]에/
냉동고[냉동실]에 넣다
put ~ in the refrigerator
[fridge]/freezer

~를 냉장 보관하다
keep ~ in the
refrigerator,
keep ~ refrigerated

~를 냉동 보관하다
keep ~ in the freezer,
keep ~ frozen

~를 냉장고[냉장실]/
냉동고[냉동실]에서 꺼내다
take ~ out of the
refrigerator[fridge]/freezer

~를 냉동하다
freeze ~

~를 해동하다
defrost ~

쌀을 씻다
wash rice

쌀을 물에 불리다
soak rice
in water

채소를 씻다
wash vegetables

채소를 다듬다, 손질하다
cut the ends off the vegetables,
clean vegetables

고기에서 기름을 떼어 내다
trim the meat

SENTENCES TO USE

그는 사 온 식품을 바로 냉장고에 넣었다.
He immediately put the food he had bought in the refrigerator.

이 제품은 냉동 보관해야 한다.　　　　This product needs to be kept frozen.

나는 고기를 냉동실에서 꺼내어 해동했다.
I took the meat out of the freezer and defrosted it.

쌀을 씻어서 물에 불려 두었다.　　　　I washed the rice and soaked it in water.

우리 어머니는 밭에서 뜯어 온 채소를 다듬으셨다.
My mother cut the ends off the vegetables she had gathered from the field.

생선을 손질하다
clean a fish
생선 내장을 빼다
gut a fish

상한 부분을 도려내다
remove[cut out]
the rotten part

껍질을 벗기다
peel

자르다, 썰다
cut

~을 토막 내다
cut ~ into
pieces

고기나 생선의 뼈나
가시를 발라내다
fillet

잘게 썰다
chop

채썰다
julienne,
shred

얇게 썰다
slice (thinly),
cut ~ into (thin) slices

깍둑썰기하다
dice, cube,
cut ~ into
cubes

다지다, 고기를 갈다
mince, finely chop

갈다, 빻다
grind

강판에 갈다
grate

즙을 짜다
squeeze

SENTENCES TO USE

생선 손질하는 건 어렵다.
It's hard to clean a fish.

고등어는 두 토막 내 주세요.
Cut the mackerel into two pieces, please.

김밥에 넣을 당근은 채썰어야 해요.
You have to shred carrots for kimbap.

카레에 넣을 감자는 깍둑썰기해 주세요.
Cut the potatoes into cubes for the curry, please.

만두를 만들기 위해 고기를 다졌다.
I minced the meat to make dumplings.

생강을 강판에 갈아서 생강차를 만들었다.
I made ginger tea by grating ginger with a grater.

2 음식 조리

MP3 029

밥을 짓다, 밥을 하다
cook rice,
make rice

김치를 담그다
make kimchi

소금에 절이다
salt

소금에 절인
salted

피클을 만들다
pickle

피클로 만든
pickled

양념에 재워 두다
marinate

양념에 재워 둔
marinated

양념하다, 무치다
season

양념한
seasoned

찌다
steam

채소를 데치다
blanch

끓이다, 삶다
boil

약한 불로 끓이다
simmer

부치다, 기름에 굽다
fry

기름에 튀기다
deep-fry

SENTENCES TO USE

그는 난생 처음 밥을 해 보았다.
He cooked rice for the first time in his life.

김치를 담그는 일은 생각보다 어렵지 않았다.
Making kimchi wasn't as hard as I thought.

한국인들은 갈비를 양념에 재워 뒀다가 요리한다.
Koreans marinate ribs before cooking them.

나는 된장과 참기름을 넣어 나물을 무쳤다.
I seasoned the vegetables with soybean paste and sesame oil.

달걀은 15분 정도 삶아.
Boil the eggs for about 15 minutes.

오징어를 통째로 튀겨 본 적 있어요?
Have you ever deep-fried a whole squid?

볶다
stir-fry

뒤집다
flip

(빵을) 굽다
bake

(오븐이나 불에) 굽다
roast

(석쇠나 그릴에) 굽다
grill

고기를 통째로 굽다,
직화로 굽다
barbecue

젓다, 섞다
stir

섞다, 버무리다
mix

으깨다
mash

(달걀 등을) 휘저어 거품을 내다
whisk

SENTENCES TO USE

양파와 파프리카, 소시지를 볶다가 케첩을 넣어서 맛을 내요.
Stir-fry onion, paprika, and sausage and then add ketchup to taste.

부침개를 깔끔하게 뒤집는 건 쉽지 않다.　　　It's not easy to flip a Korean style pancake neatly.

오븐에 구운 쇠고기와 그릴에 구운 쇠고기 중 어느 걸 더 좋아해요?
Which do you prefer, a roast or grilled beef?

삶은 감자를 으깨서 마요네즈, 소금, 후추와 함께 버무리세요.
Mash boiled potatoes and mix with mayonnaise, salt, and pepper.

달걀에 기름과 식초를 넣고 한참 휘저으면 마요네즈가 된다.
Add oil and vinegar to the eggs and whisk for a while, and you will have mayonnaise.

붓다
pour

뿌리다
sprinkle

(버터, 잼 등을) 펴 바르다
spread

달걀을 깨다
crack[break] an egg

밀가루를 반죽하다
make dough from flour

반죽을 치대다
knead dough

반죽을 발효시키다
let dough rise

밀어서 납작하게 만들다
flatten

쿠키 틀을 사용하다
use a cookie cutter

SENTENCES TO USE

파스타 위에 파슬리 가루를 뿌리면 보기 좋다.
Sprinkling parsley powder over the pasta looks good.

그 아이는 달걀을 생전 처음 깨 보았다.　　　The child broke an egg for the first time in her life.

반죽을 30분 정도 치대야 해요.
You have to knead the dough for about 30 minutes.

반죽을 1시간씩 2번 발효시키세요.　　　Let the dough rise twice, an hour each time.

나는 별 모양 쿠키 틀을 사용했다.　　　I used the star-shaped cookie cutter.

3 주방 용품, 조리 도구 사용

MP3 030

가스 불을 줄이다/키우다
turn down/up
the gas

가스를 차단하다
shut[turn] off the gas

가스레인지를 켜다/끄다
turn on/off the gas stove

가스 밸브를 잠그다/열다
close/open the gas valve

밥솥으로 밥을 하다
cook rice in a rice cooker

전자레인지에 ~를 데우다
heat ~ in the microwave

토스트를 굽다
make toast

오븐에 빵을 굽다
bake bread in the oven

오븐에 고기를 굽다
roast meat in the oven

에어프라이어로 ~를 요리하다/만들다
cook/make ~ in an air fryer

SENTENCES TO USE

찌개가 끓기 시작하면 불을 줄이세요.
Turn down the gas when the stew starts to boil.

가스레인지를 사용하고 나면 가스 밸브를 잠그세요.
Close the gas valve after using the gas stove.

전자레인지에 1분 정도 데워서 드세요.
Heat it in the microwave for about 1 minute before eating.

토스트를 구운 다음 버터와 잼을 발라 커피와 함께 먹었다.
After making toast, I spread butter and jam on it and had it with a cup of coffee.

에어프라이어로 기름을 사용하지 않고 튀김 요리를 만들 수 있다.
You can make fried food without using any oil in an air fryer.

주전자로/전기주전자로
물을 끓이다
boil water in a kettle/
an electric kettle

커피 메이커로
커피를 내리다
brew[make] coffee
with a coffee maker

도마에서 ~를 자르다[썰다]
cut ~ on a cutting
[chopping] board

믹서로 ~를 섞다
blend ~
in a blender

주방 저울로
~의 무게를 달다
weigh ~ on[using]
the kitchen scale(s)

체에 ~를 거르다
strain ~
through a sieve

행주로 식탁을 닦다
wipe the table
with a dishcloth

주방 후드를 켜다
turn on the kitchen
[range] hood

식기세척기에 그릇을 넣다
put ~ in the
dishwasher,
load the dishwasher

식기세척기의
전원을 켜다
turn on the
dishwasher

식기세척기를 돌리다
run the
dishwasher

앞치마를 두르다

(동작)
put on
an apron

(상태)
wear
an apron

SENTENCES TO USE

전기 주전자로 물 좀 끓여 주세요.　　Please boil some water in an electric kettle.

그녀는 도마에 대고 두부를 잘랐다.　　She cut tofu on the cutting board.

그녀는 채소와 과일을 믹서에 넣고 섞었다.　　She blended some vegetables and fruits in a blender.

주방 저울로 그 가루의 무게를 달아 보았다.　　I weighed the powder using the kitchen scale.

식기세척기에 그릇을 넣어 주렴.　　Put the bowls in the dishwasher.

UNIT 4 음식 먹기, 대접하기

식사를 하다
have a meal
아침/점심/저녁을 먹다
eat[have] breakfast/lunch/
supper[dinner]

간식을 먹다
have[eat] a snack
간식으로 ~을 먹다
eat ~ for a snack

야식을 먹다
have[eat] a late-night snack
야식으로 ~을 먹다
eat ~ for a late-night snack

음식을 덜어 먹다
put food on one's plate
and eat

음식을 나눠 먹다
share food with
others

음식을 권하다
offer food

상을 차리다
set the table

상을 치우다
clear the table

국자로 ~를 뜨다
ladle ~

주걱으로 밥을 푸다
scoop rice with a rice paddle

SENTENCES TO USE

간식으로는 토마토와 사과, 우유를 드세요.　　Eat tomatoes, apples, and milk for snacks.

나는 야식 먹는 습관을 버려야 한다.
I have to break the habit of eating late-night snacks.

전염병을 예방하려면 음식은 각자 접시에 덜어서 먹어야 한다.
To prevent infectious diseases, you should put food on your plate and then eat it.

요리가 거의 다 되었으니 상을 차려 주세요.
I'm almost done cooking, so please set the table.

조리사들이 직원들에게 국자로 국을 떠 주고 있다.　　Cooks are ladling soup for the employees.

숟가락으로 ~(음식)를 뜨다
spoon up ~,
scoop ~ with a spoon

젓가락으로
~(음식)를 집다
pick up ~ with
chopsticks

포크로 ~(음식)를 찍다
pick up food
with a fork

숟가락/젓가락/ 포크/
나이프를 사용하다
use a spoon/
chopsticks/a fork/
a knife

칼로 ~(음식)를 자르다
cut ~ with a knife

~(음식)를 씹다
chew ~   chew on ~, keep chewing ~
~(음식)를 우물거리다

~(음식)를 삼키다
swallow ~

국물을 마시다
drink the soup

~를 벌컥벌컥 마시다
gulp (down) ~

고기를 상추/깻잎에 싸 먹다
eat meat wrapped in
lettuce/perilla leaves

SENTENCES TO USE

나는 젓가락질을 잘 못해서 젓가락으로 음식을 집는 게 힘들다.
I'm not good at using chopsticks, so it's hard to pick up food with chopsticks.

나는 오른쪽 어금니가 아파서 그쪽으로는 음식을 씹지 못한다.
One of my right molars hurts, so I can't chew on that side.

음식을 삼키기 어려운 사람들도 있다.
Some people have difficulty swallowing.

한국에서는 고기를 상추와 깻잎에 싸서 먹는다.
In Korea, we eat meat wrapped in lettuce and perilla leaves.

~(음식)를 게걸스럽게 먹다, 허겁지겁 먹다
devour ~, eat greedily, gobble ~ up,
wolf ~ down, eat ~ in a hurry

~(음식)를 깨작거리다
pick at ~,
nibble at ~

쩝쩝거리다(시끄럽게 소리 내며 먹다)
eat noisily with one's mouth open,
lick[smack] one's lips while eating

~(음식)를
억지로 삼키다
choke down ~

~(음식)를 뱉다
spit out ~

냅킨으로 입을 닦다
wipe one's mouth
with a napkin

~(음식)를 내놓다
serve ~

~(음식)를 싸 주다
give ~ to take
home

SENTENCES TO USE

그는 배가 너무 고파서 허겁지겁 밥을 먹었다.
He was so hungry that he ate his meal in a hurry.

깨작거리지 말고 많이 좀 먹어.
Don't nibble at your food. Eat a lot.

그 남자는 쩝쩝거리면서 밥을 먹어서 거슬려.
The man eats noisily with his mouth open, and that's annoying.

우리 고양이는 입맛에 안 맞는 음식은 바로 뱉는다.
My cat spits out food right away if it doesn't suit her taste.

우리 엄마는 내가 엄마를 보러 갈 때마다 여러 가지 반찬을 집에 가져가라고 싸 주신다.
My mom gives me various side dishes to take home every time I go to see her.

CHAPTER

3

외식

EATING OUT

카페에서

MP3 032

마실 음료를 고르다
choose drinks[beverages]
to drink

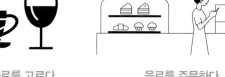

음료를 주문하다
order drinks
[beverages]

음료 값을 계산하다
pay for
the drinks

기프티콘을 음료로 교환하다
exchange a mobile
gift card[mobile gift
voucher] for a drink

기프티콘으로 음료를 구매하다
buy a drink with
a mobile gift card
[mobile gift voucher]

기프티콘 바코드를 찍다
scan the
bar code
of a mobile gift card

키오스크에서
주문하다
order from
a kiosk

전광판에서 번호를 확인하다
check the number on
the electronic display

진동벨이 울리다
a[the] pager
rings

주문한 음료를 받다
pick up the drinks

~에 시럽을 추가하다
add syrup to ~

SENTENCES TO USE

요즘은 카운터에서 음료를 주문해야 하는 카페가 많다.
These days, there are many cafes where you have to order drinks at the counter.

자리에 앉아 종업원에게 음료를 주문하는 카페도 여전히 있다.
There are still cafes where you sit down and order drinks from the staff.

나는 친구에게 선물 받은 기프티콘으로 음료를 구매했다.
I bought a drink with a mobile gift card from my friend.

진동벨이 울리면 카운터에 가서 음료를 받아 오면 된다.
When the pager rings, you can go to the counter and get the drinks.

음료를 주문한 후 주문한 음료를 받아서 자리로 가져간다.
After ordering a drink, I pick up the drink I ordered and take it to the seat.

(카페 등에서) 자리를 잡다
get a table

~를 마시다
drink ~

대화를 나누다, 수다 떨다
talk,
have a chat

커피를 마시며
over coffee

화장실을 이용하다
use the bathroom

~를 테이크아웃하다
buy ~ for takeout, order[get] ~ to go

QR코드를 찍다
check in[register] with QR codes,
scan QR codes

빈/사용한 컵과 쟁반을 반납하다
return one's empty/
used cups and trays

SENTENCES TO USE

우리는 카페에서 커피를 마시며 수다를 떨었다.　We chatted over coffee at the cafe.

그녀는 화장실을 이용하기 위해서 카페에 가서 음료를 한 잔 구입했다.
She went to a cafe and bought a drink to use the bathroom.

나는 아이스 카페라떼 한 잔을 테이크아웃했다.　I bought a glass of iced caffè latte for takeout.

요즘은 카페에 들어갈 때 QR코드를 찍어야 한다.
These days, you have to register with a QR code when entering a cafe.

그 카페를 나올 때는 빈 컵과 쟁반을 반납해야 한다.
You have to return your empty cups and trays when you leave the cafe.

MP3 033

~명 자리를 예약하다
book[reserve] a table for ~ (people),
make a reservation for ~ (people)

줄 서서 기다리다
wait in line

대기 명단에 이름을 올리다
put one's name
on the waiting list

메뉴를 고르다
choose an item from the
menu, choose a dish

종업원을 부르다
ask for[call, summon]
a server

메뉴 추천을 부탁하다
ask for a
recommendation

와인 리스트를
부탁하다
ask for
the wine list

식사를 주문하다
order a meal

식탁에 수저를 놓다
put spoons and
chopsticks on the table

잔에 물을 따르다
pour a glass of
water

SENTENCES TO USE

나는 그 식당에 전화로 6명 자리를 예약했다.   I called the restaurant and booked a table for six.

그 식당은 인기가 많아서 줄 서서 기다려야 해요.
That restaurant is so popular that you have to wait in line.

나는 그 식당에서 대기 명단에 이름을 올리고 30분쯤 기다렸다.
I put my name on the waiting list at the restaurant and waited for about half an hour.

나는 식당에서 메뉴를 고르는 게 쉽지 않다.   It's not easy for me to choose a dish at a restaurant.

그는 음식을 기다리면서 식탁에 수저를 놓고 잔에 물을 따랐다.
Waiting for food, he put spoons and chopsticks on the table and poured glasses of water.

여분의 접시/앞접시[개인접시]를
부탁하다
ask for extra/
individual plates

음식을 추가로 주문하다
order more[extra]
food

고기를 굽다

(오븐에)
roast meat

(석쇠나 불판에)
grill meat

고기를 뒤집다
turn the meat over

고기를 가위로 자르다
cut meat with
(kitchen) scissors

스테이크를 썰다
cut steak,
slice steak

스파게티를 포크에 돌돌 말다
wrap spaghetti
around a fork

음식 사진을 찍다
take pictures
[photos] of food

음식을 흘리다
spill food

물을 쏟다
spill water

음식에서 머리카락을
발견하다
find a hair
in the food

음식에 관해
불평하다
complain
about food

SENTENCES TO USE

우리는 식당 종업원에게 앞접시를 부탁했다.　　　We asked the restaurant worker for individual plates.

한국에서는 고기를 구울 때 가위로 자른다.
In Korea, when we grill meat, we cut the meat with scissors.

스파게티는 포크에 돌돌 말아서 먹는 거래.
They say we should wrap the spaghetti around a fork to eat it.

많은 사람들이 음식 사진을 찍어서 SNS에 올린다.
Many people take pictures of food and post them on SNS.

오늘 식당에서 식사를 하는데 음식에서 머리카락이 나왔다.
I was eating at the restaurant today and found a hair in the food.

남은 음식을 포장해서
집에 가져가다/가져오다
pack the leftovers and
take/bring them home

화장실을 이용하다
use the bathroom

계산서를 요청하다
ask for the bill

음식값을 계산하다
pay the bill,
pay for the meal

더치페이하다(각자 내다)
go Dutch

반반씩 내다
pay half and half,
pay fifty-fifty

여럿이 나눠서 내다
split the bill

QR코드를 찍다
check in[register] with
QR codes, scan QR codes

음식을 포장 주문하다
order ~ for takeout,
order[get] ~ to go

전화로 음식을 주문하다
order food
by phone

배달앱으로 음식을 주문하다
order food through
a (food) delivery app

SENTENCES TO USE

식당에서 남은 음식을 포장해서 집에 가져왔다.
I packed the leftovers from the restaurant and brought them home.

그 식당은 음식값 계산이 선불이다.
We have to pay for the meal in advance at the restaurant.

친구들과 만나서 식사를 하면 우리는 음식값을 나눠서 낸다.
When I meet my friends and have a meal, we split the bill.

나는 엄마를 드리려고 같은 음식을 하나 더 포장 주문했다.
I ordered one more of the same dish for takeout for my mom.

요즘은 배달앱으로 음식을 주문하는 사람들이 많다.
Many people order food through delivery apps these days.

I BOUGHT a glass of iced caffè latte
FOR TAKEOUT.

CHAPTER

4

주

HOUSE

MP3 034

잠자리에 들다
go to bed,
go to sleep

(옆자리 사람에게)
잘 자라고 인사하다
say good night to ~

~시로 알람을 맞추다
set the alarm for ~

(수면용) 안대를 하다
wear
a sleep mask

잠 못 들고 뒤척이다
toss and turn

잠들다
fall asleep

잠을 자다
sleep

똑바로 누워서 자다
sleep on
one's back

옆으로 누워서 자다
sleep on
one's side

자면서 몸을 뒤척이다
turn over
in one's sleep

잠꼬대를 하다
talk in one's sleep

코를 골다
snore

자면서 이를 갈다
grind one's teeth
in one's sleep

SENTENCES TO USE

내일 일찍 나가야 해서 알람을 5시로 맞췄다.
I set the alarm for 5 o'clock because I have to leave early tomorrow.

나는 보통 옆으로 누워서 잔다.   I usually sleep on my side.

너 어젯밤에 잠꼬대하더라.
You were talking in your sleep last night.

우리 남편은 코를 심하게 골아요.   My husband snores loudly.

내 동생은 자면서 이를 간다.   My brother grinds his teeth in his sleep.

침대를 정리하다
make one's bed

방바닥에 이부자리를 펴다
spread the[one's] bedding on the floor

이부자리를 개다
fold up the bedding

이불을 덮다
cover oneself with bedclothes [blanket]

(자면서) 이불을 차다
kick the blanket out (while sleeping)

침대 시트를 갈다
change the bed, change the sheets

베개 커버를 갈다
change the pillowcase

잠에서 깨다
wake up

잠자리에서 일어나다
get up, get out of bed

(자다가) 침대에서 떨어지다
fall[roll] off the bed while sleeping

알람을 끄다
turn off the alarm

기지개를 켜다
stretch (one's body)

하품하다
yawn

잠옷을 입다/벗다
put on/take off one's pajamas

~(옷)을 입다
put on ~

SENTENCES TO USE

매일 침대를 정리해야지.
You should make your bed every day.

우리 할머니는 주무시려고 방바닥에 이부자리를 펴셨다.
My grandmother spread her bedding on the floor to go to sleep.

베개 커버를 얼마나 자주 갈아요?
How often do you change the pillowcase?

그녀는 잠자리에서 일어나서 기지개를 켰다.
She got out of bed and stretched.

그는 잠옷을 벗고 옷을 입었다.
He took off his pajamas and put on his clothes.

2 장소별 행동 ② – 거실, 서재

MP3 035

휴식을 취하다
relax,
take[have] a rest

소파에 눕다
lie on the sofa[couch]

창밖을 내다보다
look out (of) the window

책을 읽다
read a book

그림을 그리다
draw[paint] a picture

피아노/기타를 연주하다
play the piano/guitar

SENTENCES TO USE

그녀는 퇴근 후에는 거실에서 TV를 보며 느긋하게 쉰다.
After work, she relaxes by watching TV in the living room.

지난 일요일, 나는 하루 종일 소파에 누워 TV를 보았다.
Last Sunday, I lay on the sofa watching TV all day long.

우리 고양이는 캣타워에 앉아서 거실 창밖을 내다보는 걸 좋아한다.
My cat likes to sit on the cat tree and look out the living room window.

그는 주말에는 서재에서 책을 읽거나 그림을 그린다.
He reads books or draws pictures in the study on weekends.

맨손체조를 하다
do free-hand exercises

요가를 하다
do[practice] yoga

인터넷 서핑을 하다
surf the Internet

컴퓨터로/노트북에 글을 쓰다
write on
a computer/laptop

SNS를 하다
spend time on social media,
post comments/pictures on
+ 특정 SNS 이름

TV/영화/넷플릭스/유튜브를 보다
watch TV/a movie/Netflix/YouTube (videos)

SENTENCES TO USE

나는 매일 거실에서 맨손체조를 한다.
I do free-hand exercises in the living room every day.

나는 서재에서 인터넷 서핑을 하거나 넷플릭스를 보면서 시간을 보낸다.
I spend my time surfing the Internet or watching Netflix in my study.

그녀는 매일 몇 시간을 SNS를 하면서 보낸다.
She spends several hours on social media every day.

그는 퇴근 후 저녁을 먹으면서 유튜브 동영상을 본다.
He watches YouTube videos while having dinner after work.

요리하다, ~(음식)를 만들다
cook, make[cook] ~

빵을 굽다
bake bread

커피를 내리다
brew coffee, make coffee

도시락을 싸다
pack a lunch (box)

식탁을 차리다
set the table

~(음식)을 먹다
eat ~

아침/점심/저녁 식사를 하다
eat[have] breakfast/
lunch/supper[dinner]

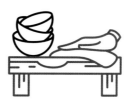

식탁을 치우다
clear the table

설거지하다
wash[do] the dishes

SENTENCES TO USE

나는 얼마 전부터 빵을 굽기 시작했다.
I started baking bread a while ago.

그녀는 아침에 일어나면 제일 먼저 커피를 내린다.
When she wakes up in the morning, she makes coffee first.

나는 요즘 아침마다 도시락을 싼다.
These days, I pack a lunch every morning.

식사를 끝내면 바로 설거지를 하는 게 좋다.
After finishing the meal, you should wash the dishes right away.

식기세척기의 전원을 켜다
turn on the dishwasher

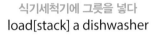
식기세척기에 그릇을 넣다
load[stack] a dishwasher

식기세척기를 돌리다
run the dishwasher

냉장고를 정리하다, 청소하다
clean the[one's]
refrigerator

음식물 쓰레기를 처리하다
dispose of food waste

주방 후드를 켜다
turn on the kitchen[range] hood

SENTENCES TO USE

내가 요리를 하고, 남편이 식탁을 치우고 식기세척기를 돌린다.
I cook, and my husband clears the table and runs the dishwasher.

정기적으로 냉장고를 청소해야 한다.
You have to clean your refrigerator regularly.

음식물 쓰레기를 처리하는 게 설거지보다 더 귀찮다.
Disposing of food waste is more of a hassle than washing dishes.

요리를 할 때는 주방 후드를 켜도록 해.
Turn on the kitchen hood when you cook.

4 장소별 행동 ④ – 욕실

MP3 **0 3 7**

손을 씻다
wash one's
hands

세수하다
wash one's
face

양치질하다
brush one's
teeth

치실질을 하다
floss (one's teeth),
use dental floss

치간 칫솔을 쓰다
use an
interdental
(tooth)brush

면도하다
shave

머리를 감다
wash one's hair

머리를 말리다
dry one's hair

머리를 빗다
comb[brush]
one's hair

머리를 손질하다(직접)
do one's hair

샤워하다
take[have]
a shower

목욕하다
take[have]
a bath

욕조에 물을 받다
fill the
bathtub

스킨/로션/크림을 바르다
apply[put] toner/
lotion/cream
(on one's face)

바디 로션을 바르다
apply[put]
body lotion
(on one's body)

SENTENCES TO USE

외출했다 돌아오면 바로 손을 씻어야지.
You should wash your hands as soon as you get back.

치실질을 하거나 치간 칫솔을 쓰세요.   Floss or use an interdental toothbrush.

머리는 밤에 감는 게 더 좋다.   It's better to wash your hair at night.

보니는 데이트가 있어서 머리를 손질했다.   Bonnie had a date, so she did her hair.

샤워는 미지근한 물로 하는 게 더 좋다.   It's better to take showers with lukewarm water.

피부가 건조하면 바디 로션을 꼭 바르세요.   If your skin is dry, make sure to apply body lotion.

손톱/발톱을 깎다
cut[clip] one's
nails/toenails

염색하다(직접)
dye one's hair

화장하다
put on makeup

화장을 지우다
remove (one's)
makeup

오줌을 누다, 소변을 보다
go to the bathroom, pee(아이들 말),
do[go, make] number one,
urinate(의료·생물학 용어)

똥을 누다, 대변을 보다
go to the bathroom,
poop(아이들 말), do[go, make]
number two, defecate(의료·생물학 용어)

비데를 사용하다
use a bidet

**변기의 물을
내리다**
flush
the toilet

막힌 변기를 뚫다
unclog
a toilet

욕실 청소를 하다
clean
the bathroom

욕조를 청소하다
clean
the (bath)tub

**휴지걸이에
새 휴지를 걸다**
put a new roll of
paper in the holder

SENTENCES TO USE

나는 손톱을 너무 짧게 깎았다.
I cut my nails too short.

그는 머리를 파란색으로 염색했다.
He dyed his hair blue.

화장은 하는 것보다 지우는 게 중요하다는 말이 있다.
There is a saying that it is more important to remove makeup than to put on makeup.

공중 화장실에서 변기 물 내리는 걸 잊는 사람들이 있다.
There are people who forget to flush the toilet in public restrooms.

최소 1주일에 한두 번 욕실 청소를 하지 않으면 곰팡이가 핀다.
If you don't clean the bathroom at least once or twice a week, you'll get mold.

MP3 038

세탁물을 분류하다
sort the laundry

흰 빨랫감과 색깔 있는
빨랫감을 분리하다
separate the colors
from the whites

빨래하다, 세탁하다
wash the clothes,
do the laundry

세탁기를 돌리다
do the laundry
using the
washing machine

세탁기에 빨래를 넣다
load the washing machine,
put the laundry in the
washing machine

세제/섬유유연제를 넣다
add detergent/
fabric softener

세탁기에서 빨래를 꺼내다
unload the washing machine,
take the laundry out of the
washing machine

(건조대에/빨랫줄에) 빨래를 널다
hang (out) the laundry
(on a clothes drying rack/clothesline)

빨래를 걷다
get the laundry,
take the laundry off the clothesline

건조기를 돌리다
run a clothes
dryer

세탁조를 청소하다
clean the washing
machine tub

SENTENCES TO USE

세탁기 덕분에 빨래하는 게 정말 쉬워졌다.
The washing machine made it really easy to do the laundry.

흰 빨랫감과 색깔 있는 빨랫감을 분리해서 세탁해야 한다.
You have to separate the colors from the whites and then wash it.

세탁기가 다 돌아가면 세탁기에서 빨래 좀 꺼내 주세요.
Please take the laundry out of the washing machine when the cycle is finished.

비가 와서 빨래를 방에 있는 건조대에 널었다.
It rained, so I hung out the laundry on the clothes drying rack in the room.

비가 오기 시작해서 마당의 빨랫줄에서 빨래를 걷었다.
It started to rain, so I took the laundry off the clothesline in the yard.

식물/꽃/채소를 키우다
grow plants/
flowers/
vegetables

식물/꽃/채소에 물을 주다
water the plants/
flowers/vegetables

베란다를 물청소하다
clean the balcony
with water

베란다를 홈카페로 꾸미다
decorate the balcony like a cafe,
make the balcony as a coffee nook

* 베란다? 발코니?
우리나라의 아파트나 빌라에서 흔히
'베란다(veranda)'라고 부르는 공간은 대부분
의 경우 '발코니(balcony)'라고 하는 게 더
적절하다. 베란다는 아래층과 위층의 면적
차이로 인해 생기는 공간을 말하기 때문이다.

창고에 물건을 보관하다
store things in the
storage room

창고에 ~를 넣다
put ~ in the storage room

창고에 ~를 쌓아 두다
pile ~ up in the storage room

창고에서 ~를 꺼내다
take ~ out of the storage room

SENTENCES TO USE

우리 엄마는 베란다에서 화초를 많이 키운다.
My mom grows many plants and flowers on the balcony.

나는 올해에 베란다에서 채소를 키울 거야.
I'm going to grow vegetables on the balcony this year.

나는 오늘 베란다 물청소를 했다.   I cleaned the balcony with water today.

우리는 창고에 안 쓰는 물건과 선풍기, 휴지 등을 보관한다.
We store unused items, electric fans, tissues, etc. in the storage room.

청소기를 창고에 넣어 두렴.   Put the vacuum in the storage room.

주차하다 park, park a car	주차장에서 차를 빼다 take the car out of the parking lot	차고 문을 열다/닫다 open/close the garage door	손세차하다 hand-wash one's car	바비큐 파티를 하다 have a barbecue (party)

나무/꽃을 심다/기르다 plant/grow trees/flowers	텃밭에 채소를 기르다 grow vegetables in the vegetable[kitchen] garden	식물/꽃/채소에 물을 주다 water the plants/ flowers/vegetables	텃밭에 비료를 주다 fertilize the vegetable garden

채소를 따다, 뜯다 pick (the) vegetables	마당에 조경 공사를 하다 do landscaping work in the yard	정원에 잔디를 깔다 turf the garden, lay the garden with turf	잔디를 깎다 mow the lawn	잡초를 뽑다 weed, pull (up) weeds

SENTENCES TO USE

그는 집에서 차를 직접 손세차한다.
He hand-washes his car himself at home.

지난 토요일에 옥상에서 친구들과 바비큐 파티를 했다.
I had a barbecue party with my friends on the rooftop last Saturday.

모니카는 텃밭에서 여러 가지 채소를 기른다.
Monica grows various vegetables in the vegetable garden.

요즘 비가 안 와서 텃밭의 채소에 물을 줘야 한다.
It hasn't rained lately, so I have to water the vegetables in the kitchen garden.

나는 텃밭의 채소를 따다가 샐러드를 만든다.
I pick vegetables in the kitchen garden and make a salad.

7 집 청소, 기타 집안일

MP3 040

집 청소

집을 청소하다
clean
the house

청소기를 돌리다
vacuum the floor,
run the vacuum cleaner

청소기를 충전하다
charge the
vacuum cleaner

빗자루로 쓸다
sweep ~

낙엽을 갈퀴로
긁어모으다
rake (the)
leaves

바닥을 (대)걸레질하다
mop the floor,
run a mop over the floor

손걸레로 ~를 닦다
wipe ~ with a rag
[with wet cloth]

걸레를 빨다
wash
a mop[rag]

돌돌이로 반려동물의
털을 제거하다
remove pet hair with
a lint roller

창틀의 먼지를 닦다
wipe the dust off
the window frames

욕실 청소를 하다
clean the
bathroom

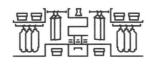

옷장/서랍을 정리하다
organize[clean out]
one's closet/drawer

신발장을 정리하다
arrange
one's shoe rack
[shoe closet]

SENTENCES TO USE

이틀에 한 번은 청소기를 돌려야 한다.
I have to vacuum the floor once every other day.

그는 마당의 낙엽을 긁어모았다.　　　　He raked the leaves in the yard.

바닥을 대걸레로 닦아야 해요.　　　　　You have to mop the floor.

걸레로 탁자와 책상 위를 닦으세요.　　　Wipe the table and desk with a rag.

나는 돌돌이로 우리 고양이의 털을 계속 제거해야 한다.
I have to keep removing my cat's hair with a lint roller.

쓰레기통을 비우다
empty the
waste basket
[trash can]

쓰레기를 분류하다
sort garbage
[waste]

쓰레기를/재활용
쓰레기를 내다버리다
take out the garbage
[waste]/recyclables

재활용 쓰레기를 분리 (배출)하다
separate the recyclables
and the trash, sort the
recyclables

그 외의 집안일

일주일치 식단을 짜다
plan a week's
meals

장보기 목록을 작성하다
make a grocery list

장을 보다
do (the, one's) shopping

식료품 장을 보다
do grocery shopping

~를 다림질하다
iron ~

반려동물을 돌보다
take care of pets

SENTENCES TO USE

네 방 쓰레기통 좀 비워.   Empty the waste basket in your room.

쓰레기는 일반 쓰레기, 음식물 쓰레기, 재활용 쓰레기로 분류해야 한다.
Garbage should be sorted as general waste, food waste, and recyclables.

우리 아파트에서는 재활용 쓰레기를 금요일에 버려야 한다.
In my apartment building, we have to take out the recyclables on Fridays.

장 볼 목록을 작성하면 시간이 절약되고 불필요한 소비를 피하는 데 도움이 된다.
Making a grocery list saves you time and helps you avoid buying things unnecessarily.

퇴근길에 식료품 장을 보았다.   I did grocery shopping on my way home from work.

셔츠와 블라우스 다림질하는 게 집안일 중에 시간을 제일 잡아먹는다.
Ironing shirts and blouses is the most time-consuming chore.

8 가전제품 사용

MP3 041

~(가전제품)를 설치하다
install ~

전등을
켜다/끄다
turn on/off the light

컴퓨터/노트북을 켜다/끄다
turn on/off the
computer/laptop

TV를 켜다/끄다
turn on/off
the TV

(TV) 채널을 ~로 돌리다
change
the channel to ~

TV의 볼륨을
키우다/줄이다
turn up/down
the TV (volume)

냉장고 문을 열다/닫다
open/close the
refrigerator (door)

냉장고의 온도를 조절하다
adjust[control]
the temperature
on the refrigerator

인덕션을 켜다/끄다
turn[switch] on/off
the induction
cooktop[stove]

인덕션의 온도를 조절하다
adjust[control] the
temperature on the induction
cooktop[stove]

주방 후드를 켜다/끄다
turn[switch] on/off the
kitchen[range] hood

SENTENCES TO USE

필요 없는 전등은 끄세요.
Turn off the lights you don't need.

채널 좀 다른 데로 돌려 봐.
Change the channel.

TV 볼륨 좀 줄이세요.
Please turn down the TV volume.

냉장고 온도를 좀 조절해야겠어요.
I need to adjust the temperature on the refrigerator.

인덕션 켜는 법을 모르겠어요.
I don't know how to turn on the induction cooktop.

전자레인지에
~를 데우다
heat ~ in the
microwave

정수기로 물을 받다
get water from a
water purifier

전기주전자로
물을 끓이다
boil water in an
electric kettle

에어프라이어로
음식을 만들다
cook[make] ~
in[with] an air fryer

에어컨을 세게 틀다(온도를 내리다)
turn up the air conditioner

에어컨을 약하게 틀다(온도를 올리다)
turn down the air conditioner

에어컨을 켜다/끄다
turn on/off
the air conditioner

선풍기를 켜다/끄다
turn[switch]
on/off the electric fan

보일러/난방기를 세게 틀다(온도를 올리다)
turn up the boiler/heater

보일러/난방기를 약하게 틀다(온도를 내리다)
turn down the boiler/heater

보일러/난방기를 켜다/끄다
turn on/off the boiler/heater

SENTENCES TO USE

그건 전자레인지에 4분 정도 데우렴.
Heat it in the microwave for about 4 minutes.

에어프라이어로 튀김 만들어 봤어요?
Have you ever made fried food in an air fryer?

너무 더워요. 에어컨 좀 세게 틀어 주세요.
It's too hot. Please turn up the air conditioner.

슬슬 보일러를 켤 계절이 오네요.
The season to turn on the boiler is coming.

실내가 덥네요. 난방기 온도 좀 내려 주세요.
It's hot in here. Please turn down the heater.

가습기를 틀다/끄다
turn on/off the
humidifier

제습기를 틀다/끄다
turn on/off the
dehumidifier

공기청정기를 틀다/끄다
turn on/off the
air purifier

헤어드라이어로 머리를 말리다
dry one's hair with
a hair dryer

~(가전제품)를
렌탈하다
rent ~

A/S(애프터서비스)를 신청하다
call the after-sales service[customer
service] number (to get[have] ~ fixed)

~(가전제품)의 A/S(애프터서비스)를 받다
have ~ serviced

~(가전제품)의 수리를 받다
have[get] ~ fixed

폐가전제품 수거를 신청하다
arrange to have an old
appliance picked up

SENTENCES TO USE

겨울에는 실내가 건조해서 가습기를 틀어야 한다.
In winter, the room is dry, so I have to turn on the humidifier.

요리하고 나서는 환기시킨 후에 공기청정기를 가동해야 한다.
After cooking, you should turn on the air purifier after airing out the room.

요즘은 정수기와 공기청정기 같은 가전제품을 렌탈해서 쓰는 사람들도 많다.
Nowadays, many people rent home appliances such as water purifiers and air purifiers.

냉장고에 문제가 생겨서 A/S를 신청했다.
There was a problem with the refrigerator, so I called the after-sales service number.

나는 못 쓰게 된 세탁기의 수거를 신청했다.
I have arranged to have my old washing machine picked up.

집을 수리하다, 보수하다
repair[renovate] the[one's] house

집을 개조하다, 리모델링하다(다른 형태로 만들다)
remodel the[one's] house

집의 인테리어를 새로 하다
(도배, 페인트칠 등을 새로 하다)
redecorate the[one's] house

집수리 견적서를 받다
get an estimate
for home repairs

베란다를 트다/거실을 확장하다
remove[get rid of] the balcony/
widen the living room

베란다에 인조잔디를 깔다
install artificial grass[turf]
on the balcony

SENTENCES TO USE

올 봄에 집을 보수하려고 해요.
I'm going to renovate my house this spring.

그 사람은 집을 리모델링해서 팔았대요.
They say he remodeled and then sold his house.

집이 오래돼서 인테리어를 새로 해야 해요.
My house is old, so I have to redecorate it.

그 아파트는 베란다를 없애서 거실이 넓은데, 나는 베란다가 있는 집이 좋다.
The apartment has a large living room because the balcony was removed, but I like
an apartment with a balcony.

집에 단열 공사를 하다
insulate a house

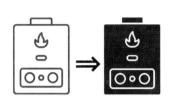

보일러를 교체하다
replace the boiler

옥상을/지붕을 방수 처리하다
waterproof the rooftop/roof

마루를 새로 깔다
redo the floor, lay a new floor

(방을) 새로 도배하다
put up new wallpaper (in a room)

SENTENCES TO USE

우리 집 보일러가 고장 나서 교체해야 한다.
My boiler is broken, so I have to replace it.

우리는 10년 만에 옥상을 다시 방수 처리했다.
We waterproofed the rooftop again after 10 years.

바닥을 다시 까실래요? 원목 바닥은 어떠세요?
Do you want to redo the floor? How about wood flooring?

우리는 이사 들어가기 전에 도배를 새로 했어요.
We put up new wallpaper before we moved in.

장판을 새로 깔다
lay new linoleum

벽난로를 설치하다
install a fireplace

수도 배관을 교체하다
replace water pipes

창틀을[새시를] 교체하다
replace window frames

욕실 타일을 교체하다
retile the bathroom

욕조를 설치하다
install a bathtub

욕조를 뜯어내고
샤워부스를 설치하다
remove a bathtub and
install a shower stall

샤워 헤드를 교체하다
change[replace]
a shower head

곰팡이를 제거하다
remove[get rid of]
mold

SENTENCES TO USE

부모님 댁의 창틀이 낡아서 교체해 드렸다.
I had the window frames of my parents' house replaced because they were old.

욕실에 욕조를 설치하고 싶다.
I want to install a bathtub in the bathroom.

이 세제로 욕실 타일의 곰팡이를 제거할 수 있어요.
You can remove mold from bathroom tiles with this detergent.

전구를 갈다
change[replace] a light bulb

거울을 바꿔 달다
change[replace] a mirror

LED등으로 교체하다
switch to LED lights

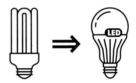

형광등을 LED등으로 교체하다
replace fluorescent lights with LED lights,
change fluorescent lights to LED lights

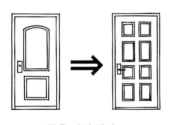

문을 바꿔 달다
replace a door

문고리를 바꿔 달다
replace a doorknob

SENTENCES TO USE

전구를 가는 건 제가 직접 할 수 있어요.
I can change the light bulb myself.

형광등을 LED등으로 교체하는 붐이 일었다.
There was a boom in replacing fluorescent lights with LED lights.

내 방 문의 문고리가 고장 나서 교체했다.
The doorknob of my room was broken, so I replaced it.

CHAPTER

5

건강, 질병

HEALTH & DISEASE

눈물을 흘리다
shed tears

눈곱이 끼다
have[get] some
sleep[sand, gunk]
in one's eyes

하품하다
yawn

배에서 꼬르륵 소리가 나다
one's stomach growls

딸꾹질하다
hiccup

기침하다
cough

재채기하다
sneeze

트림하다
burp, belch

방귀 뀌다
fart, pass gas

땀을 흘리다
sweat

식은땀을 흘리다
break out in
a cold sweat

콧물을 흘리다
have a runny nose,
one's nose runs

SENTENCES TO USE

아침에 일어나면 눈곱이 많이 껴 있다.
I have a lot of gunk in my eyes when I wake up in the morning.

편두통을 앓을 때는 자꾸 하품이 나올 수 있다.   When you have a migraine, you might yawn a lot.

그는 알레르기가 있어서 계속 재채기를 한다.   He keeps sneezing because of allergies.

다른 사람들과 식사를 하면서 트림을 하는 건 예의에 어긋나는 행동이다.
It's not polite to burp while eating with others.

그녀는 갱년기에 접어든 후로 땀이 많이 난다.
She's been sweating a lot since she reached menopause.

오줌을 누다, 소변을 보다
go to the bathroom, pee
(아이들 말), do[go, make] number
one, urinate(의료·생물학 용어)

똥을 누다, 대변을 보다
go to the bathroom, poop
(아이들 말), do[go, make] number
two, defecate(의료·생물학 용어)

생리를 하다, 생리 중이다
have a period,
be on one's period

생리통이 있다
have cramps,
have menstrual
[period] pain

생리전증후군으로
고생하다
suffer from PMS
(premenstrual syndrome)

혈압이 올라가다
one's blood
pressure rises

혈압이 내려가다
one's blood
pressure goes down

갈증이 나다
feel[be]
thirsty

졸리다
feel[be]
drowsy

졸음이 쏟아지다
nearly fall
asleep

눈이 감기다
be so sleepy one can't
keep one's eyes open

SENTENCES TO USE

엄마, 나 쉬하고 올게.
Mom, I'm going to pee.

지금 생리 중이라서 컨디션이 좀 안 좋아요.
I'm not feeling well because I'm on my period.

내 여동생은 생리통이 심하다.
My sister has severe menstrual pain.

나는 두통이 오면 혈압이 내려가요.
My blood pressure goes down when I get a headache.

어젯밤에 잠을 거의 못 잤더니 졸음이 쏟아져요.
I hardly slept last night, so I'm nearly falling asleep.

MP3 **044**

몸이 아프다
be sick,
be ill

~가 아프다
~ hurt(s)
~에 통증이 있다
have a pain in ~

통증을 견디다
bear
[tolerate]
the pain

두통/복통/요통/치통/생리통이 있다
have a headache/a stomachache/
a backache/a toothache/menstrual
pain[period pain, menstrual cramps]

어깨가 결리다, 뻐근하다
one's shoulders are stiff, have stiff
shoulders, feel stiff in the shoulders

목이 아프다
have a sore throat

목이 뻣뻣하다, 뻐근하다
one's neck is stiff

눈이 따끔거리다
one's eyes
smart[sting]

눈이 간지럽다
one's eyes are
itchy

코가 막히다
have a stuffy[stuffed]
nose, one's nose is
stuffed up[stuffy]

입술이 트다, 갈라지다
one's lips are[get]
chapped

SENTENCES TO USE

몇 시간 동안 걸었더니 발이 아프다.
My feet hurt because I walked for hours.

그는 어젯밤부터 치통이 있다.
He has had a toothache since last night.

노트북 앞에서 작업을 오래 했더니 어깨가 뻐근하다.
My shoulders are stiff because I worked in front of my laptop for a long time.

알레르기 때문에 눈이 간지럽다.
My eyes are itchy because of allergies.

겨울에는 날씨가 건조해서 나는 입술이 잘 튼다.
My lips get chapped easily in winter because the weather is dry.

(손발이) 저리다
be numb, go numb

다리가/관절이/무릎이 쑤시다
one's leg/joint/knee is sore,
one's leg/joint/knee aches

다리가 저리다
have pins and needles in one's leg,
one's leg is numb, have no feelings in one's leg,
one's leg falls asleep

약을 복용하다
take medicine

~ 약을 복용하다
take ~ medicine

진통제/감기약/소화제/항생제/수면제를 복용하다
take a painkiller/cold medicine/
digestant[digestive medicine]/
antibiotics/a sleeping pill

알약/물약/가루약을 복용하다
take a pill[tablet]/liquid medicine/
powdered medicine

SENTENCES TO USE

우리 할머니는 비가 오면 무릎이 쑤신다고 하신다.
My grandmother says her knees ache when it rains.

그녀는 생리통이 있어서 약을 먹었다.
She took medicine because she had menstrual pain.

그 아이는 가루약을 잘 못 먹는다.
The child has difficulty taking powdered medicine.

그는 고질적인 두통 때문에 진통제를 자주 복용한다.
He often takes painkillers because of his chronic headaches.

~를 다치다
get hurt on ~,
hurt ~, injure ~

~에서 피가 나다
~ is bleeding

무릎이 까지다
scrape one's knee,
have one's knee skinned[scraped]

~를 치료받다
have one's ~ treated,
be treated for ~,
get treatment for ~

상처를 소독하다
disinfect a wound

~에 연고를 바르다
apply ointment[salve] to ~,
put[rub in] ointment[salve] on ~

~에 밴드를 붙이다
apply a Band-Aid to ~,
put a Band-Aid on ~

SENTENCES TO USE

그 남자는 자전거를 타다가 넘어져서 다리를 다쳤다.
The man fell while riding a bicycle and hurt his leg.

내 동생이 넘어져서 무릎이 까졌다.
My brother fell and scraped his knee.

그녀는 허리 통증 치료를 꾸준히 받고 있다.
She has been getting ongoing treatment for back pain.

그는 상처에 연고를 바르고 밴드를 붙였다.
He applied ointment to the wound and put a Band-Aid on it.

~에 붕대를 감다
apply[put]
a bandage to ~

~에 깁스를 하다
wear[apply] a cast
to[on] ~

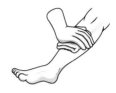

지혈하다
stop the bleeding

~를 냉찜질하다
cool ~, put an ice[a cold] pack on ~

~를 온찜질하다
put a hot pack on ~

침을 맞다
get acupuncture

지압을 받다
get acupressure

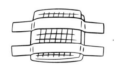

상처를 거즈로 덮다
cover the wound with
a piece of gauze

~에서 고름을 짜다
squeeze the pus
from[out of] ~

SENTENCES TO USE

그녀는 발목뼈가 부러져서 깁스를 했다.
She broke her ankle and wore a cast.

상처에서 피가 계속 나서 지혈을 해야 했다.
The wound kept bleeding, so I had to stop the bleeding.

부은 부위에는 냉찜질을 하면 좋다.
It's good to put cold packs on swollen areas.

우리 할머니는 허리가 아프면 침을 맞으신다.
My grandmother gets acupuncture when her back hurts.

~의 딱지를 떼다
pick the scab from ~

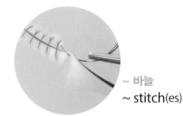

~ 바늘
~ stitch(es)

상처를 봉합하다, 꿰매다
suture a wound

흉터가 남다
have a scar,
a scar is left

손목/발목을 삐다
sprain one's
wrist/ankle

뼈가 부러지다
break a bone,
~ bone is broken

응급 치료를 받다
receive first aid (treatment),
receive emergency treatment

인공호흡을 하다
give someone
mouth-to-mouth

심폐소생술을 실시하다
do CPR
(cardiopulmonary resuscitation)

SENTENCES TO USE

그 아이는 넘어져서 이마가 찢어졌고, 10바늘을 꿰매야 했다.
The child fell and cut his forehead, and required 10 stitches.

나는 어렸을 때 넘어져서 생긴 흉터가 무릎에 있다.
I have a scar on my knee that I got as a child from falling down.

그 노인은 빙판에 미끄러져 넘어져서 고관절이 부러졌다.
The old man slipped and fell on the ice and broke his hip.

나는 지하철에서 쓰러진 사람에게 인공호흡을 해 주었다.
I gave mouth-to-mouth to the person who collapsed on the subway.

3 병원 – 진료, 검사

MP3 045

병원에 진료 예약을 하다
make[schedule] an
appointment with
a doctor

진료를 받다
go see a doctor
치료를 받다
get medical treatment

체온을 재다
take[check] one's
temperature

혈압을 재다
take[check] one's blood pressure

맥박을 재다
take[check] one's pulse

채혈하다
have[get] blood taken

혈액 검사를 받다
take[have, get]
a blood test

소변 검사를 받다
take[have, get]
a urine test

X선 검사를 받다
take[have, get]
an X-ray

SENTENCES TO USE

몸이 안 좋을 때는 병원에 가서 진료를 받으세요.
When you're not feeling well, go see a doctor.

그는 고혈압 약을 먹기 시작한 후로 혈압을 매일 재 왔다.
He has checked his blood pressure every day since he started taking high blood pressure pills.

내 맥박을 재 보았더니 1분에 90번이나 되었다.
I took my pulse, and it reached 90 beats a minute.

오늘 병원에서 혈액 검사와 X선 검사를 받았다.
I had a blood test and an X-ray at the hospital today.

초음파 검사를 받다
take[have, get] an ultrasound

복부/유방 초음파 검사를 받다
take[have, get] an abdominal/a breast ultrasound

유방 X선 촬영을 하다
get a mammogram

자궁 경부암 검사를 받다
get a Pap smear test

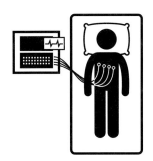

심전도 검사를 받다
take[have, get] an
ECG(electrocardiogram)

SENTENCES TO USE

나는 1년에 한 번씩 유방 초음파 검사를 받는다.
I take a breast ultrasound once a year.

유방 X선 촬영을 할 때는 유방에 통증이 다소 느껴진다.
When I get a mammogram, I feel some pain in my breast.

나는 오늘 병원에서 심전도 검사를 받고 심박동기 점검을 받았다.
I had an ECG and had my pacemaker checked at the hospital today.

CT 촬영을 하다
have[get, do]
a CT scan

MRI 검사를 받다
have[get, do]
an MRI

위/대장 내시경
검사를 받다
have[get] a
gastroscopy/
colonoscopy

용종을 떼어내다
have a polyp
removed

(~의) 조직 검사를 받다
have[get, take]
a ~ biopsy

분변 검사를 하다
have[get]
scatoscopy

B형 간염 검사를 받다
get tested for
hepatitis B

구강 검사를 받다
get a dental
checkup

시력/청력 검사를 하다
have one's eyesight/
hearing tested

~라고 진단받다
be diagnosed
with ~

~(약)을 처방받다
be prescribed ~

주사를 맞다
get a shot,
get an injection

~ 예방 접종을 하다,
~ 백신을 맞다
get vaccinated
against ~

정기 검진을 받다
have[get]
a regular
checkup

SENTENCES TO USE

그는 머리가 자주 아파서 뇌 MRI 검사를 받았다.　　He had a brain MRI because he often had headaches.

위 내시경 검사는 최소 2년에 한 번은 받아야 한다.
You should get a gastroscopy at least once every two years.

나는 작년에 유방암 조직 검사를 받았으나 다행히 암이 아닌 것으로 나왔다.
I had a breast biopsy last year, but fortunately it came back negative for cancer.

그는 40대 초반에 고혈압으로 진단받았다.
He was diagnosed with high blood pressure in his early forties.

나는 어제 코로나바이러스 백신을 맞았다.
I got vaccinated against COVID-19 yesterday.

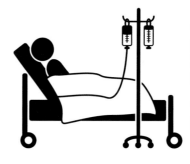

입원하다
be hospitalized,
be admitted to (the) hospital

입원 중이다
be in the hospital

입원 수속을 하다
go through the
hospitalization process

수술 일시를 잡다
schedule surgery[an operation],
set a date and time for surgery[an operation]

수술 동의서에 서명하다
sign the surgery
consent form

수술 전 주의 사항을 듣다
listen to the precautions
before surgery

(~ 동안) 금식하다
fast (for ~)

수술실로 옮겨지다
be taken to the
operating room

SENTENCES TO USE

그는 항암 화학 치료를 위해 입원했다.
He was hospitalized for chemotherapy.

우리 어머니는 심장 판막 수술 일시를 잡았다.
My mother scheduled a heart valve operation.

수술 전에 12시간은 금식해야 한다.
You have to fast for 12 hours before surgery.

마취가 되다
be anesthetized

마취에서 깨어나다
wake up from anesthesia

~ 수술을 받다
have[get] ~ surgery
[a(n) ~ operation]

개복/가슴 절개 수술을 받다
have[get] an open abdominal/
open chest surgery

복강경/내시경 수술을 받다
have[get] laparoscopic/
endoscopic surgery

* surgery와 operation

surgery : '수술'이라는 행위를 추상적 개념으로 나타냄. 보통 셀 수 없는 명사.
operation : 구체적인 한 건 한 건의 수술을 나타냄. 셀 수 있는 명사.

SENTENCES TO USE

나는 수술 후 회복실에서 마취에서 깨어났다.
I woke up from anesthesia in the recovery room after the surgery.

그녀는 작년 봄에 위암 수술을 받았다.
She had gastric cancer surgery last spring.

복강경 수술은 개복 수술보다 회복이 더 빠르다.
If you have laparoscopic surgery, you will recover faster than if you have an open
abdominal surgery.

수혈을 받다
have[get, receive,
be given] a blood transfusion

수술 후 회복실/일반 병실로 옮겨지다
be taken to the recovery room/
general ward after surgery

~ 수술 후 회복하다
recover from ~ surgery
[a(n) ~ operation]

혼수상태에 빠지다
fall into a coma

수술 후 실밥을 제거하다
have stitches removed
after surgery

수술 후 가스를 배출하다
fart[pass gas,
break wind] after surgery

SENTENCES TO USE

그 환자는 수술 중에 수혈을 받아야 했다.
The patient had to get a blood transfusion during surgery.

그는 치질 수술을 받고 회복 중이다.
He's recovering from a hemorrhoids operation.

안타깝게도 그 환자는 수술 중에 혼수상태에 빠졌다.
Unfortunately, the patient fell into a coma during surgery.

수술 후 가스를 배출하는 건 좋은 징조다.
It's a good sign when you pass gas after some surgeries.

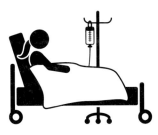

정맥[링거] 주사를 맞다
get an IV (injection[shot]),
get an intravenous shot

약을 복용하다
take medicine,
take a(n) ~ pill

퇴원 수속을 밟다
go through the discharge
procedure

퇴원하다
be discharged
(from (the) hospital),
leave (the) hospital

보험회사 제출용 서류를 발급 받다
be issued documents
to submit to the insurance company

다음 진료를 예약하다
schedule a doctor's
appointment

SENTENCES TO USE

나는 입원 기간 내내 정맥 주사를 맞았다.
I got IV injections throughout my hospital stay.

그 환자는 하루 세 번 식후에 약을 복용하고 있다.
The patient is taking medicine three times a day after meals.

그녀는 입원 생활 2개월 만에 어제 퇴원했다.
She was discharged yesterday after two months in the hospital.

그녀는 퇴원하면서 보험회사에 제출할 서류를 발급받았다.
When she was discharged from the hospital, she was issued documents to submit to the
insurance company.

MP3 047

다이어트하다,
식이 요법을 하다
be on a diet

다이어트를
시작하다,
식이 요법을
시작하다
go on
a diet

체중을 감량하다
lose weight

다이어트 식단을 짜다
plan a diet

소식하다
eat little,
eat like a bird

저녁을 굶다
skip dinner

1일 1식을 하다
eat one
meal a day

1일 1식 다이어트를 하다
be on an OMAD diet

거식증에 걸리다
get anorexia, suffer from
anorexia, be anorexic

저탄고지 다이어트를 하다
be on an LCHF
(low carbohydrate high fat) diet

원푸드 다이어트를 하다
be on a mono diet,
be on a single-food diet

간헐적 단식을 하다
be on an
intermittent diet

한약으로 살을 빼다
lose weight with
herbal medicine

SENTENCES TO USE

그 배우는 1년 내내 다이어트를 한다.
The actress is on a diet all year round.

그녀는 체중을 감량해야 한다고 늘 말한다.
She always says she needs to lose weight.

그는 1일 1식을 한 지 1년이 넘었다고 한다.
He is said to have been eating one meal a day for more than a year.

저탄고지 다이어트를 하는 사람들이 적지 않다.
More than a few people are on an LCHF diet.

원푸드 다이어트는 건강에 좋지 않은 것 같다.
I don't think a single-food diet is good for your health.

식욕 억제제를
복용하다
take an appetite
suppressant

지방흡입술을 받다
have[get, undergo]
liposuction

치팅 데이를 갖다
have a cheat day

요요 현상이 오다
have a yo-yo effect

운동하다
work out, exercise,
get some exercise(s)

규칙적으로/꾸준히 운동하다
work out regularly/steadily
땀복을 입고 운동하다
work out in a sauna suit
유산소 운동을 하다
do aerobic exercise(s)

매일 체중을 재다
weigh oneself every day

BMR - Basal
Metabolic Rate

신진대사를 촉진하다
boost metabolism

기초 대사율을 높이다
increase the basal
metabolic rate

근육량을 늘리다
increase muscle
mass

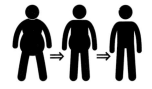

체지방을 줄이다
reduce body fat

SENTENCES TO USE

그 사람은 복부 지방흡입술을 받았다.　　　The man had abdominal liposuction.

그녀는 다이어트 중이라 일주일에 한 번 치팅 데이를 가져서 그날 먹고 싶은 걸 먹는다.
She's on a diet, so she has a cheat day once a week and eats what she wants that day.

운동을 많이 해도 식이 요법을 하지 않으면 살이 빠지지 않는다.
Even if you work out a lot, you won't lose weight without going on a diet.

살을 빼려면 유산소 운동을 해야 한다.　　　You have to do aerobic exercise to lose weight.

살을 빼고 유지하려면 신진대사를 촉진하고 근육량을 늘려야 한다.
If you want to lose weight and maintain it, you should boost metabolism and increase
your muscle mass.

6 죽음

MP3 048

사고로/병으로/노환으로 죽다
die in an accident/from an illness/of old age

고독사하다
die alone

고독사
solitary death, lonely death

죽다, 세상을 떠나다
die, pass away

* pass away는 die의 완곡한 표현으로,
'돌아가시다, 세상을 떠나시다'로 번역할 수 있다.

자살하다,
스스로 목숨을 끊다
kill oneself,
commit suicide

시신을 영안실에 안치하다
place a dead body in a mortuary

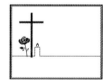

~의 부고를 내다
send an obituary of ~

A에게 B의 죽음을 알리다
inform A of B's death

시신을 염습하다
wash and dress a corpse for burial

SENTENCES TO USE

그의 아버지는 작년에 세상을 떠나셨다.
His father passed away last year.

알베르 카뮈는 46세의 나이에 교통사고로 세상을 떠났다.
Albert Camus died in a car accident at the age of 46.

그 나라에서는 2021년에 고독사한 사람이 3,159명에 달했다.
In that country, 3,159 people died alone in 2021.

2020년 그 나라에서는 하루에 약 36명이 스스로 목숨을 끊었다.
In that country in 2020, about 36 people killed themselves a day.

입관하다
place the body in the coffin

장례식을 하다
hold[conduct] a funeral

조문객을 맞이하다
greet mourners

조문하다, 조의를 표하다
express one's condolences on the death of ~

조의금을 전달하다
offer condolence money

조의 화환을 보내다
send
a funeral wreath

SENTENCES TO USE

그 추기경의 장례식은 그 도시에서 가장 큰 성당에서 열렸다.
The cardinal's funeral was held in the city's largest cathedral.

고인의 부인과 어린 아들이 조문객을 맞이하고 있었다.
The deceased's wife and young son were greeting mourners.

우리는 그녀의 아버지가 돌아가신 것에 조의를 표했다.
We expressed our condolences on the death of her father.

그 언론인의 아버지 장례식에 많은 정치가들이 조의 화환을 보냈다.
Many politicians sent funeral wreaths to the journalist's father's funeral.

발인하다
carry a coffin out of the house[funeral hall]

영정(사진)을 들다
carry a picture of the deceased

관을 운구차에 싣다
load a coffin into the hearse

시신을 매장하다
bury a body

시신을 화장하다
cremate a body

유골함을 들다
carry a burial urn

유골을 납골당에 안치하다
place somebody's remains in a charnel house

유골을 뿌리다
scatter someone's ashes

수목장을 하다
bury someone's ashes under a tree,
have someone's ashes buried under a tree

~의 사망 신고를 하다
report someone's death

SENTENCES TO USE

그는 돌아가신 할아버지의 영정을 들고 운구 행렬의 맨 앞에서 걸었다.
He led the funeral procession carrying a picture of his deceased grandfather.

그의 시신은 화장한 후 납골당에 안치됐다.
His body was cremated and placed in a charnel house.

그녀는 자신의 유골을 바다에 뿌려 달라고 했다.
She asked to have her ashes scattered at sea.

요즘은 수목장을 원하는 사람들이 많다.
These days many people want to have their ashes buried under a tree.

제사를 지내다
have[hold] an ancestral rite

추모제를[추도식을] 열다
hold[have] a memorial service

성묘하다, 묘지를 방문하다
visit someone's grave
(and have a memorial service there)

SENTENCES TO USE

점점 더 많은 집들이 제사를 간소하게 지낸다.
More and more families hold simple ancestral rites.

오늘 그 사고 희생자들을 위한 추모제가 열렸다.
Today, a memorial service was held for the victims of the accident.

그는 짐 모리슨의 무덤에 가 보기 위해 파리로 여행 갔다.
He traveled to Paris to visit Jim Morrison's grave.

PART III

사회생활 속

행동 표현

EMOTIONS & RELATIONSHIP

기쁨의 눈물을 흘리다
shed tears of joy,
cry happy tears,
weep for joy, cry with joy

(~에) 열광하다
go wild[crazy, mad]
(about ~), get wildly
excited (about ~)

환호하다
cheer,
shout with joy

환호하며 박수 치다
cheer and
clap

환호하며 맞이하다
greet ~ with
loud cheers

~를 반기다
welcome ~,
be delighted to see[meet] ~

~를 환대하다, 귀빈 대접을 하다
show[extend, offer] hospitality to ~,
treat ~ like royalty

칭찬하다
praise, compliment

반응하다, 리액션하다
show a reaction

SENTENCES TO USE

결승선을 1등으로 통과한 선수는 기쁨의 눈물을 흘렸다.
The athlete who crossed the finish line first shed tears of joy.

그 밴드가 무대에 등장하자 팬들은 열광했다.
When the band appeared on the stage, the fans went wild.

그 영화가 아카데미 작품상을 수상했다는 소식에 모두 환호했다.
Everyone cheered at the news that the film had won the Academy Award for Best Picture.

그는 자신을 찾아온 친구를 반갑게 맞았다.   He welcomed a friend who was visiting him.

그녀는 사람들을 칭찬하는 데 소질이 있다.   She has a knack for praising people.

화내다
get angry[mad,
furious], lose
one's temper

짜증내다
throw
a tantrum,
get irritated

심술부리다
do something
mean, act surly

~와 눈을 마주치지 않다
not make eye contact with ~,
not look someone in the eye,
avoid making eye contact with

화를 벌컥 내다
fly into a rage,
fly off the handle

악을 쓰다
scream like
hell

(절망, 분노 등으로)
머리를 쥐어뜯다
tear one's
hair out

하염없이 울다
cry one's eyes out
(눈이 빠질 정도로 운다는 의미)

(화가 나서)
발을 구르다
stomp one's
foot (in anger)

주먹으로 책상을 내리치다
pound[hit] the desk
with one's fist

비난하다
denounce,
condemn

혼내다
scold,
call down

(~을) 욕하다
swear (at ~),
curse (at ~)

(~에게) 사과하다
apologize
(to ~)

SENTENCES TO USE

그녀는 그의 무책임한 행동에 화를 냈다.
She got angry at his irresponsible behavior.

나는 이틀 연속 잠을 거의 못 자서 사람들에게 짜증을 냈다.
I slept very little for two days in a row and got irritated with people.

그녀가 노크를 하지 않고 방문을 열자 그는 화를 벌컥 냈다.
He flew into a rage when she opened the door without knocking.

사고로 목숨을 잃은 그 아이의 어머니는 하염없이 눈물을 흘렸다.
The mother of the child, who lost his life in the accident, cried her eyes out.

그 남자는 청문회에서 주먹으로 책상을 내리치면서 고함을 쳤다.
The man screamed at the hearing as he pounded the desk with his fist.

눈물을 흘리다
shed tears,
weep

틀어박혀 있다
shut oneself in,
stay indoors

경청하다
listen (to ~),
be all ears

위로하다
console, comfort,
cheer ~ up

격려하다
encourage

~를 배려하다
be considerate to ~

아부하다, 아첨하다
flatter

질투하다
get jealous

무시하다, 얕보다
look down on, belittle

경멸하다
despise, scorn

비웃다
laugh at, make fun of,
ridicule, mock

잘난 체하다
put on airs

SENTENCES TO USE

그녀는 무기력감에 빠져서 이틀간 자기 방에 틀어박혀 있었다.
Feeling lethargic, she shut herself in her room for two days.

대화의 기본은 상대방의 이야기를 경청하는 것이다.
The basis of conversation is to listen to the other person.

어린 딸아이가 그녀를 위로해 주었다.
A young daughter comforted her.

그는 항상 남들을 배려하려 노력한다.
He always tries to be considerate to others.

그녀는 자기보다 아래에 있다고 생각하는 사람들을 무시하는 경향이 있다.
She tends to look down on people who she thinks are beneath her.

MP3 050

친해지다
get[become] close (to ~),
make friends (with ~),
become intimate (with ~)

사이좋게 지내다
get along (well)
(with ~)

어울려 다니다
run around (with ~)

(남녀가) 사귀다
go out (with ~),
date (~)

말다툼하다
have an argument (with ~),
have words (with ~),
argue[quarrel] (with ~)

싸우다
argue[quarrel]
(with ~), fight (with ~)

사이가 멀어지다
grow apart (from ~),
be estranged (from ~)

냉대하다
give the
cold
shoulder
(to ~)

화해하다
make up (with ~), make peace (with ~),
reconcile (with ~)

화해를 청하다
ask for
reconciliation

A와 B 사이를 이간질하다
drive a wedge between A and B,
turn A against B

SENTENCES TO USE

우리는 같은 회사에서 일하면서 친해졌다.
We became close while working at the same company.

그는 같은 반 친구들과 모두 사이좋게 지낸다.   He gets along well with all his classmates.

그녀는 오늘 남자 친구와 말다툼을 했다.
She had an argument with her boyfriend today.

나는 언제부턴가 그녀와 사이가 멀어졌다.   I've been estranged from her for some time.

그는 데이비드와 그의 상사 사이를 이간질했다.
He drove a wedge between David and his boss.

~에게 반하다
have a crush on ~

눈이 높다
have high
standards

~를 좋아하다
have feelings for ~

~에게 마음이 있다
have a thing for ~

~와 썸 타다
have a thing
with ~

~에게
데이트 신청을 하다
ask ~ out (on a date)

~와 사귀다, 데이트하다
go out with ~,
date ~

밀당하다, 튕기다
play hard to get

~ 동안 사귀다
be together for ~

~와 헤어지다
break up with ~

다시 만나다
get back together

SENTENCES TO USE

나는 버스 정류장에서 자주 보는 그 남자에게 반했다.
I have a crush on the man I often see at the bus stop.

요즘 썸 타는 사람 없어?　　　　　Is there anyone you have a thing with?

지금 사귀는 사람은 없어요.　　　　I'm not dating anyone right now.

나는 밀당 같은 건 안 해.　　　　　I don't play hard to get.

그 두 사람은 2년 정도 사귀었어.
The two have been together for about two years.

~를 차다
dump ~, kick ~

~를 두고 바람피우다
cheat on ~

사랑싸움을 하다
have a lovers' quarrel

~와 약혼하다
get engaged to ~

~에게 청혼하다
propose to ~

~와 결혼하다
marry ~,
get married to ~

이혼하다
get divorced, get a divorce

~와 이혼하다
divorce ~

SENTENCES TO USE

그 여자는 남자 친구를 차고 다른 남자에게 갔다.
She dumped her boyfriend and went to another man.

그 가수는 아내를 두고 바람을 피웠다.   The singer cheated on his wife.

그들은 걸핏하면 사랑싸움을 했다.   They often had lovers' quarrels.

나는 다정한 사람과 결혼하고 싶다.   I want to marry a friendly person.

그 글로벌 기업의 CEO는 아내와 결혼 생활 27년 만에 이혼했다.
The CEO of the global company divorced his wife after 27 years of marriage.

CHAPTER

2

일, 직업

WORKS & JOBS

(~로) 통근하다
commute (by ~)

출근하다
go to work,
go to
the office

퇴근하다
leave work, get off work,
leave the office,
be gone for the day

출근 카드를 찍다
clock in, punch in

퇴근 카드를 찍다
clock out,
punch out

회의하다
have a
meeting

업무를 할당하다
assign work

업무 보고를 하다
give a report
of the work

서류 작업을 하다
do paperwork

보고서를 작성하다
make[write]
a report

결재 서류를 올리다
submit documents for
(someone's) approval

기획서를 쓰다/제출하다
write/submit
a project proposal

프레젠테이션을 하다
give
a presentation

SENTENCES TO USE

나는 지하철로 통근한다.
I commute by subway.

노동자들은 교대 근무가 시작될 때와 끝날 때 출퇴근 카드를 찍는다.
The workers clock in and out at the start and end of each shift.

우리 팀은 매일 아침 회의를 하고, 우리 부서는 일주일에 한 번 회의를 한다.
Our team has a meeting every morning, and our department has a meeting once a week.

나는 시장 조사 결과에 대해 보고서를 작성해야 한다.
I have to write a report on the results of the market research.

그는 그 기획안에 대해 프레젠테이션을 했다.
He gave a presentation on the project proposal.

거래처에 전화하다
call a client

전화를 받다
answer the
call[phone],
take the call[phone]

전화를 (다른 사람에게)
돌리다
transfer a call

회사 인트라넷에
접속하다
access the
company's Intranet

이메일을 확인하다
check one's
email

이메일을 보내다
send
an email

이메일에
답장을 보내다
reply to an email

팩스를 보내다/받다
send/receive
a fax

프린터로 출력하다
print out

복사하다
xerox,
photocopy

고객을 만나다
meet one's
client

~로 출장을 가다
go on[take, be on]
a business trip to ~

해외 출장을 가다
go on an overseas
business trip

상사에게 혼나다, 깨지다
be chewed out
by one's boss

SENTENCES TO USE

오늘은 거래처에 전화할 일이 많았다.   I called clients many times today.

전화를 받아서 담당자에게 돌려 주었다.
I answered the phone and transferred it to the person in charge.

모두가 인터넷을 사용하는 요즘에도 사람들이 팩스를 보낼 때가 가끔 있다.
Even today, when everyone just uses the Internet, there are still times people send faxes.

나는 이번 주에 부산으로 출장을 간다.   I'm going on a business trip to Busan this week.

그는 상사에게 혼나서 기분이 좋지 않다.   He is not happy as he was chewed out by his boss.

휴가를 내다[쓰다]
take a day off[time off, a PTO(personal time off)]
병가를 내다
take sick leave, take a sick day
연차 휴가를 내다[쓰다, 가다]
take annual[yearly] leave, go on annual leave

여름휴가를 가다
go on[take] a summer
holiday[vacation]

초과 근무를 하다
work overtime

초과 근무 수당을 받다
get overtime pay, get paid overtime

휴일에 근무하다
work on a holiday

회사에 지각하다
be late for work

시말서를 제출하다
submit a written apology (and explanation)

SENTENCES TO USE

오늘 병원 진료 예약이 있어서 하루 휴가를 냈다.
I took a PTO today for a doctor's appointment.

그는 오늘 아침에 감기 기운이 있어서 병가를 냈다.
He felt like he had a cold this morning, so he took a sick day.

요즘은 초과 근무를 하면 초과 근무 수당을 받아요.
These days, if I work overtime, I get overtime pay.

내가 젊을 때는 초과 근무는 물론이고 휴일에도 일을 했었다.
When I was young, I worked not only overtime but also on holidays.

그 사건으로 그는 시말서를 제출했다.
He submitted a written apology for the incident.

회식을 하다
get together (with coworkers)
for dinner or drinks

연봉 협상을 하다
negotiate for one's annual salary

월급을 받다
get[draw] a salary, get paid

급여가 오르다
get a pay raise

급여가 깎이다
get a pay cut

SENTENCES TO USE

팀원들은 어제 신입사원을 환영하기 위해 저녁에 회식을 했다.
The team members got together for dinner yesterday to welcome the new employee.

나는 연봉 협상을 해서 급여가 조금 올랐어요.
I negotiated for my annual salary and I got a small pay raise.

나는 매달 25일에 월급을 받는다.
I get paid on the 25th of every month.

상여금을 받다, 보너스를 받다
get[receive] a bonus

가불을 하다
get an advance,
get[draw, receive] (액수)
in advance

재직증명서를 떼다
get a copy of one's
certificate[proof]
of employment

신입사원을 모집하다
recruit new
employees[workers]

신입사원을 채용하다
hire[engage] new
employees[workers]

신입사원을 교육시키다
train new
employees[workers]

수습 기간을 보내다
have[go through]
a probation period

전문성[직무 능력]을 개발하다
do professional
development

사직서를 내다
hand in one's
notice[resignation]

SENTENCES TO USE

올해에는 회사 매출이 좋아서 우리는 연말 상여금을 넉넉히 받았다.
The company's sales were good this year, so we received a generous year-end bonus.

비자를 신청하려면 재직증명서를 떼야 합니다.
To apply for a visa, you must get a copy of your certificate of employment.

그 회사에서 신입사원을 모집하고 있다.　　　　The company is recruiting new employees.

신입사원들은 3개월의 수습 기간을 보낸다.
New employees have a three-month probation period.

후임자에게 업무를[맡은 일을] 인계하다/설명하다
hand over/explain one's duties
[responsibilities] to one's successor

퇴사하다
resign
(from a company)

승진하다 　　 ~로 승진하다
be[get] promoted, 　 be[get]
get a promotion 　 promoted (to ~)

이직하다
change one's job,
move to another company

해고당하다
get[be] fired, get[be] laid off

퇴직하다, 은퇴하다
retire (from ~)

SENTENCES TO USE

퇴사하기 전에 후임자에게 맡은 일을 설명해야 합니다.
You need to explain your responsibilities to your successor before leaving the company.

그녀는 지난달에 팀장으로 승진했다.
She was promoted to team leader last month.

나는 내년에 다른 회사로 옮길 거야.
I will move to another company next year.

그 사람은 교직에서 은퇴한 후 그림을 그리기 시작했다.
After retiring from teaching, he began drawing.

MP3 053

(매일 아침) 매장 문을 열다,
영업을 시작하다
open the store

(매일 저녁) 매장 문을 닫다,
영업을 끝내다
close the store

고객을 맞이하다
greet[meet]
customers

고객 문의에 응대하다
respond to
customer inquiries

주문을 받다
take an order

(점원이) 상품을 계산하다
ring up

~(상품)를
포장해 주다
wrap ~

고객의 요구에 응하다
meet the needs
of customers

번호를/이름을 부르다
call the
number/name

잘못된 주문을 처리하다
handle[deal with]
wrong orders

포인트를 적립하다
earn[collect] (reward/
bonus) points

고객의 불만에 응대하다
respond to customer
complaints

SENTENCES TO USE

그들은 오전 10시에 매장 문을 연다.
They open the store at 10 a.m.

그 직원은 항상 웃는 얼굴로 고객을 맞이한다.
The employee always greets customers with a smile.

고객 문의에 응대하다 보면 하루가 금방 지나간다.
The day flies by when I'm responding to customer inquiries.

나는 그 슈퍼마켓에서 물건을 사면 항상 포인트를 적립한다.
I always earn reward points when I buy things at the supermarket.

전화를 받다
answer[get] a call

콜센터에 전화하다
call a customer service center

문의 사항을 청취하다
listen to inquiries

상담을 해 주다(정보나 조언을 주다)
provide information
or advice

담당 부서로 전화를 돌리다
transfer a call to the
department in charge

통화 내용을 녹음하다
record phone conversations

필요한 후속 조치를 취하다
follow up on the necessary measures,
take necessary follow-up measures

SENTENCES TO USE

그 콜센터 상담원은 하루에 80통 정도의 전화를 받는다고 한다.
The call center agent is said to get about 80 calls a day.

전화를 받으면 고객의 문의 사항을 잘 청취해야 한다.
When you answer a call, you should listen to the customer's inquiries carefully.

그는 전화를 담당 부서로 돌렸다.
He transferred the call to the department in charge.

그녀는 고객과 통화한 후 필요한 후속 조치를 취했다.
She talked to the customer and followed up on the necessary measures.

3 제조업

MP3 054

통근버스를 타고 출퇴근하다
take a commuter bus to and from work,
go to and from work by commuter bus

사원증을 찍다
scan employee
ID card

보안/안전 점검을 하다
conduct a security/
safety check

작업복으로 갈아입다
change into one's work
clothes[workwear]

방진복/방진화/장갑/마스크를 착용하다
wear dustproof clothes/
dustproof shoes/gloves/masks

에어 샤워를 하다
take an air shower

기계를 점검하다
check[inspect]
a machine

제품을 검수하다
inspect products

불량품을 잡아내다
pick out defective
products

2/3교대로 일하다
work in two/three
shifts

SENTENCES TO USE

그는 통근버스를 타고 출퇴근한다.
He takes a commuter bus to and from work.

그들은 사원증을 찍고 건물에 들어간다.
They scan their employee ID card when they enter the building.

그들은 근무 중에 장갑을 끼고 마스크를 써야 한다.　They have to wear gloves and masks while on duty.

반도체 공장에서는 청정실에 들어가기 전에 에어 샤워를 해야 한다.
In a semiconductor factory, they have to take an air shower before entering a clean room.

그들은 3교대로 일한다.　　　　　　　　　They work in three shifts.

잔업을 하다, 특근을 하다
work overtime,
work extra hours

휴식 시간을 갖다
have a break

구내식당에서 점심을 먹다
have[eat] lunch
in the cafeteria

공장 기숙사에서 살다[지내다]
live in a factory
dormitory

~에게 업무를 인계하다
hand over one's
duties[responsibilities] to ~

현장 시찰단을 안내하다
guide the field
inspection team

업무상 재해를 입다
be[get] injured in a workplace
accident, have an accident at work,
have a workplace accident

노조를 결성하다
form a labor
union

노사 협의가 결렬되었다
the talks between
labor and management
broke down

파업하다
go on
strike

SENTENCES TO USE

수주량이 많아서 이번 달에는 다들 잔업을 많이 했다.
Everyone worked overtime a lot this month because of the high volume of orders.

보통 나는 구내식당에서 아침과 점심을 먹는다.
Usually I have breakfast and lunch in the cafeteria.

그녀는 공장 기숙사에서 생활한다.
She lives in a factory dormitory.

그 사람은 업무상 재해를 입었다.
The man was injured in a workplace accident.

노사 협의가 결렬되어 노동자들은 파업에 돌입했다.
The talks between labor and management broke down and the workers went on strike.

농업

벼/배추/콩… 농사를 짓다
farm rice/Chinese
cabbage/beans …

경운기로/트랙터로 땅을 갈아엎다
work the land with
a cultivator/tractor

논에 물을 대다
irrigate
a rice paddy

모판을 준비하다
prepare
seedbeds

모내기를 하다, 모를 심다
plant rice,
plant young rice plants

이앙기를 사용하다
use a rice planting
machine

비료를 주다
fertilize

항공 방제
(농약 공중 살포)를 하다
crop-dust

벼를 베다, 추수하다
harvest rice

논에서 물을 빼다
drain a rice paddy

건조기로 쌀을 건조시키다
dry rice with
a rice dryer

정미소에서 쌀을 도정하다
dehusk rice at
a rice mill

SENTENCES TO USE

그들은 귀농하여 딸기 농사를 짓는다.　　　They took up farming and farm strawberries.

요즘은 이앙기로 모내기를 한다.
These days, people plant rice using rice planting machines.

그들은 트랙터로 논에 비료를 주고 있다.　　　They are fertilizing rice fields with a tractor.

보통 9월 말에서 10월 초에 벼를 추수한다.
They usually harvest rice from late September to early October.

쌀은 조리하기 전에 도정해야 한다.　　　You have to dehusk rice before you can cook it.

파종하다
sow seeds

모종을 심다
plant a seedling

잡초를 뽑다, 김매다
weed out, pull out weeds,
root out weeds

밭에 거름을 주다
spread manure on a field

농약을 치다
spray[dust] (agricultural) pesticide

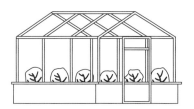

~를 (비닐) 하우스에서 재배하다
grow ~ in greenhouses

~를 수확하다
harvest ~

SENTENCES TO USE

우리 엄마는 올해에도 텃밭에 고추 모종을 심으셨다.
My mom planted pepper seedlings in her kitchen garden again this year.

밭에서 잡초를 뽑아 줘야 한다.
You have to pull out the weeds in the field.

이 상추는 농약을 뿌리지 않고 키운 것이다.
This lettuce is grown without spraying pesticides.

그들은 비닐하우스에서 귤을 재배한다.
They grow tangerines in greenhouses.

수산업

조업을 나가다
go out to the sea,
go fishing

양식을 하다, 양어장을 하다
run a fish farm,
raise fish in a fish farm

그물을 던지다
cast a net
그물을 끌어당기다
draw[haul] in a net

어선을 정박하다
anchor
a fishing boat

조업을 마치고 복귀하다
return from
fishing

잡은 해산물을 나누다/저장하다
divide/store the catch

잡은 해산물을 어시장에서 경매하다
auction the catch
at the fish market

어구를 손질하다
repair[mend]
fishing gear

SENTENCES TO USE

그 어부들은 이른 아침 해가 뜨기 전에 조업을 나간다.
The fishermen go fishing early in the morning before the sun rises.

그들은 양식으로 광어를 기른다.
They raise flatfish in a fish farm in the sea.

나는 어부들이 잡은 해산물을 어시장에서 경매하는 것을 본 적이 있다.
I have seen fishermen auction the catch at the fish market.

그 어부들은 조업을 마치고 어구를 손질하고 있다.
The fishermen have finished fishing and are repairing their fishing gear.

5 경제 활동 전반

생산하다
produce

유통시키다
distribute

소비하다
consume

판매하다
sell

구입하다
buy, purchase

**사업을 하다,
장사하다**
do business

~와 거래하다
do business
with ~

~에 투자하다
invest in ~

아르바이트를 하다
work part-time

은행에 예금하다
deposit money
in a bank

이자를 받다
earn interest

대출을 받다
get a loan

주식에 투자하다
invest in stocks

배당금을 받다
receive
a dividend

SENTENCES TO USE

그 업체에서는 국산 쌀로 만든 막걸리를 생산한다.
The company produces makgeolli made from domestic rice.

그 나라에서는 많은 양의 마늘을 소비한다.　The country consumes a lot of garlic.

그녀는 대학교 1학년 때부터 아르바이트를 해 왔다.
She has worked part-time since she was a freshman in college.

대출을 받기가 점점 더 어려워지고 있다.　It's getting harder and harder to get a loan.

요즘 많은 20대들이 주식에 투자한다.　Many people in their 20s invest in stocks these days.

CHAPTER

3

쇼핑

SHOPPING

오프라인 쇼핑 ①
– 편의점, 슈퍼마켓, 재래시장, 대형 마트

MP3 057

물건을 고르다
choose goods

물건을/가격을 비교하다
compare goods/
prices

~의 가격을 문의하다
ask the price of ~

상품에 대해 문의하다
ask about
goods[products]

~를 카트에 담다
put ~ in the cart

~를 장바구니에 담다
put ~ in the
shopping bag

~(물건) 값을 계산하다
pay for ~

가격을 흥정하다, 가격을 깎다
(상인/소비자가)
haggle over the price
(소비자가)
ask for a lower price

~를 덤으로[증정품으로] 받다
get ~ as a free gift

~를 덤으로 주다
throw ~ in

(상인이) 가격을 깎아 주다
give someone a deal

SENTENCES TO USE

나는 가격을 비교한 후에 상품을 구입한다.
I buy products after comparing prices.

대형 마트에서는 상품에 대해 문의할 직원을 찾기가 어렵다.
It is difficult to find employees to ask about products in large stores.

그는 선반의 물건들을 골라서 카트에 담았다.
He picked things off the shelves and put them in the cart.

재래시장에서 물건 값을 깎는 사람들이 있다.
There are people who haggle over the prices of goods at the traditional market.

포인트를 적립하다
earn[collect]
(reward/bonus) points

제휴 카드로 할인받다
get a discount with
a partner membership card

무빙워크를 이용하다
use a moving walkway
[moving sidewalk]

구입한 물건을 차 트렁크에 싣다
put[load] the purchased goods
[items] in the trunk of a car

구입한 물건을 배달시키다
have the purchased
goods[items] delivered

SENTENCES TO USE

그녀는 물건을 살 때마다 포인트 적립하는 걸 잊지 않는다.
She doesn't forget to earn reward points every time she buys something.

그 편의점에서는 제휴 카드로 할인을 받을 수 있다.
You can get a discount at that convenience store with a partner membership card.

구입한 물건들을 차 트렁크에 싣고 있는데 전화벨이 울렸다.
The phone rang when I was loading the purchased items in the trunk of the car.

나는 슈퍼마켓에서 산 물건들을 집으로 배달시켰다.
I had the goods I had bought at the supermarket delivered to my house.

2

오프라인 쇼핑 ②
– 각종 상점, 백화점, 면세점

MP3 058

상품을 고르다
choose goods

사이즈를 문의하다
ask about the size
(of ~)

(옷을) 입어 보다,
(신발을) 신어 보다,
(액세서리를) 착용해 보다
try on ~, try ~ on

가격을 확인하다
check the price (of ~)

가격을 문의하다
ask about the price (of ~)

~를 계산하다
pay for ~

July, 7th

배달 날짜를 정하다
set a delivery date

아이쇼핑하다
go window-shopping

DYTY FREE

~(물건)을
면세로 구입하다
buy[purchase] ~
duty free

면세점에서
~(물건)을 구입하다
buy[purchase]
~ at a duty-free shop

여권과 항공권을 제시하다
present one's
passport and
boarding pass

ICN Airport

공항에서 물건을 받다
collect the items at the
pick-up desk[counter]
at the airport

SENTENCES TO USE

나는 직원에게 원피스의 사이즈를 문의했다.
I asked the staff about the size of the dress.

바지는 사기 전에 입어 봐야 한다.
You should try on pants before buying them.

그녀는 외국 브랜드의 가방을 면세로 구입했다.
She bought a bag from a foreign brand duty free.

면세점에서는 여권과 항공권을 제시해야 한다.
We must present our passports and boarding passes at a duty-free shop.

나는 시내 면세점에서 구입한 물건을 공항 픽업 카운터에서 받았다.
I collected my purchase from the duty-free shop in the city at the airport pick-up counter.

3 미용 서비스 시설 이용

MP3 059

미용실, 마사지숍

* 이 페이지의 미용 관련 표현은 모두 헤어 디자이너가 머리를 해 줄 때의 표현.

머리를 하다
have[get]
one's
hair done

머리를 자르다[깎다]
have[get] one's
hair cut, have
[get] a haircut

머리를 짧게 자르다
have[get]
one's hair
cut short

머리를 스포츠
머리로 깎다
get a buzz cut

머리를 완전히 밀다
have[get] one's
hair shaved
completely

머리를 다듬다
have[get] one's
hair trimmed

머리를 퍼머하다
have[get] one's hair permed,
have[get] a perm

머리를 염색하다
have[get] one's
hair dyed

머리를 감다
have[get] one's
hair washed

머리를 말리다, 드라이하다
have[get] one's hair
blow-dried

머리를 하는 동안 잡지를 읽다
read a magazine while
having one's hair done

메이크업을 받다
have[get] one's
makeup done

마사지를 받다
get a massage

SENTENCES TO USE

그는 매달 머리를 깎는다.　　　　　　He gets a haircut every month.

오랜만에 머리를 자르고 퍼머를 했다.
I had my hair cut and got my hair permed after a long time.

그는 군에 입대할 때 머리를 스포츠머리로 깎았다.　He got a buzz cut when he entered the army.

나는 흰머리 때문에 한 달에 한 번 염색을 해야 한다.
I have to have my hair dyed once a month because of my gray hair.

그녀는 머리를 파란색으로 염색했다.　　　She had her hair dyed blue.

네일숍

네일을[네일 아트를] 받다
have[get] one's nails done, have[get] a manicure

네일 디자인을 고르다
choose nail designs

손톱에 젤네일을 받다
have gel nails
applied

손톱에 젤네일을
붙이다 (직접)
apply gel nails
on (finger)nails

젤네일을 제거하다
have gel nails
removed

젤네일을 제거하다 (직접)
remove[take off]
gel nails

손톱에
네일 스티커를 붙이다
put nail stickers
on (finger)nails

네일 스티커를
제거하다
remove nail
stickers

발톱에 네일을 받다
have[get] one's
toenails done

손톱/발톱을 관리 받다
have one's fingernails/
toenails cared

발 각질 케어를 받다
get the dead
skin removed
from one's feet

SENTENCES TO USE

그녀는 가끔 네일숍에서 네일을 받는다.
She sometimes gets her nails done at the nail salon.

요즘은 손톱에 젤네일을 받는 경우가 많다.
Nowadays, people often have gel nails applied.

네일숍에 가는 대신 집에서 네일 스티커를 붙이는 사람들도 많다.
Many people put nail stickers on their nails at home instead of going to the nail salon.

나는 여름에는 발톱에 네일을 받는다.　　　　I have my toenails done in summer.

그녀는 네일숍에서 발 각질 케어를 받았다.
She got the dead skin removed from her feet at the nail salon.

4 온라인 쇼핑

MP3 060

온라인
쇼핑을 하다
shop online

···에서 ~를
주문하다
order ~
at[from] …

~(제품)를
고르다
choose ~

제품/가격을
비교하다
compare
goods/prices

~를 장바구니에
넣다
add ~ to one's[the]
(shopping) cart

할인 쿠폰을 적용하다
apply a discount
coupon

배송비를 지불하다
pay for delivery,
pay for shipping

배송 주소를 입력하다
enter the shipping
address

안심번호를 사용하다
use a
"safe number"

개인통관고유부호를
입력하다
enter one's
PCCC (personal
customs clearance
code)

결제하다
make a payment

포인트(적립금)를 사용하다
use (bonus/reward) points

~를 관심 품목 리스트에 추가하다
add ~ to
one's wishlist

SENTENCES TO USE

나는 온라인 서점에서 그의 신간을 주문했다.
I ordered his new book from an online bookstore.

온라인 쇼핑을 할 때는 가격을 쉽게 비교할 수 있다.
You can easily compare prices when shopping online.

구매 금액이 5만 원 미만이면 배송비를 지불해야 한다.
If the purchase price is less than 50,000 won, you have to pay for delivery.

해외 물품을 직구할 때는 개인통관고유부호를 입력해야 한다.
When you buy overseas goods directly, you must enter your personal customs clearance code.

주문 내역을 조회하다
check the details of
an order

배송 정보를 조회하다
check the tracking
information

판매자에게 문의 글을 남기다
leave[post] a question
to the seller

배송 지연으로 판매자에게 항의하다
complain to the seller
about delayed delivery

A를 B로 교환하다
exchange A for B

~를 반품하다
return ~

환불받다
get a refund

후기를 작성하다
write a review

사진과 함께 후기를 올리다
post a review
with a photo

SENTENCES TO USE

그는 이틀 전에 주문한 운동화의 배송 정보를 조회했다.
He checked the tracking information for the sneakers he had ordered two days earlier.

나는 배송 날짜와 관련하여 판매자에게 문의 글을 남겼다.
I posted a question to the seller regarding the delivery date.

그녀는 분홍색 쿠션을 회색 쿠션으로 교환했다.   She exchanged a pink cushion for a gray one.

온라인에서 구입한 구두가 너무 작아서 반품했다.
The shoes I bought online were too small, so I returned them.

그녀는 온라인에서 구입한 원피스의 후기를 사진과 함께 올렸다.
She posted a review of the dress she had bought online along with a photo.

There are people who
haggle over the prices of goods
at the traditional market.

CHAPTER

4

출산, 육아

CHILDBIRTH & PARENTING

MP3 061

임신 테스트를 하다
take a
pregnancy test

병원에서 임신을 확인하다
confirm one's
pregnancy
at a hospital

~를 임신하다, 아이를 갖다
be pregnant (with ~),
have a baby

쌍둥이/세쌍둥이를
임신하다
be pregnant with
twins/triplets

 8 months

임신 ~주/개월이다
be ~ weeks/
months pregnant

산모 수첩을 쓰다
write in the new mother's
notebook[diary],
write in the pregnancy diary

엽산을/철분제를
복용하다
take folic acid/
iron pills

초음파 검사를 받다
get[take, have]
an ultrasound

기형아 선별 검사를 받다
get[take, have]
an abnormality
screening test

태아 염색체 검사를 받다
get[take, have] a fetal
chromosome test

임신성 당뇨병에 걸리다
suffer from
gestational diabetes

임신성 고혈압에 걸리다
suffer from gestational
hypertension

입덧을 하다
have morning
sickness

SENTENCES TO USE

나는 집에서 임신 테스트를 한 다음 병원에서 임신을 확인했다.
I took a pregnancy test at home and then confirmed my pregnancy at the hospital.

우리 언니는 쌍둥이를 임신했다.　　　　My sister is pregnant with twins.

그녀는 임신 27주다.　　　　She is 27 weeks pregnant.

임신 초기에는 태아 염색체 검사도 받아야 한다.
You also need to get a fetal chromosome test early in the pregnancy.

나는 입덧을 거의 하지 않았다.　　　　I hardly ever had morning sickness.

태교로 ~를 하다
do ~ for prenatal
education

신생아 용품을 구매하다
buy newborn baby
products

아기 방을 꾸미다
decorate
a nursery

출산 예정이다
be expecting a baby,
be due (to give birth)

진통이 있다
have labor pains,
have contractions

진통이 ~분 간격으로 있다
have contractions
[labor pains]
every ~ minutes
[~ minutes apart]

양수가 터졌다
one's water broke

분만 중이다,
진통 중이다
be in labor

~를 자연분만하다
give birth to ~ naturally,
have ~ by natural
childbirth

제왕절개로 낳다
deliver ~
by Caesarean
section

탯줄을 자르다
cut the umbilical
cord

(~를) 출산하다
give birth to ~

아기를 분만실에서
신생아실로 옮기다
move a baby from
the delivery room
to the neonatal unit

SENTENCES TO USE

그녀는 출산 전에 신생아 용품을 구매하고 아기 방을 꾸몄다.
She bought newborn baby products and decorated the nursery before giving birth.

내 딸은 다음 주에 출산 예정이다.   My daughter is due next week.

그녀는 진통 중이다.   She's in labor.

그 산모는 진통이 10분 간격으로 있다.   The mother has contractions every 10 minutes.

그녀는 오늘 여자 아기를 출산했다.   She gave birth to a baby girl today.

정부로부터 출산 축하금을 받다
get government benefits
for having a baby

난산을 하다
have a hard labor

조산하다
give birth prematurely,
have the baby arrive early

유산하다
miscarry

사산하다
have a stillbirth,
give birth to a stillborn
(baby)

아이가 생기지 않다
cannot have a baby, cannot get pregnant,
be unable to conceive

여자 쪽이/남자 쪽이 불임이다
the woman/the man
is infertile

난임 전문 병원에 다니다
go to a fertility clinic

배란일을 체크하다
check one's
ovulation day

SENTENCES TO USE

그 여성은 임신 8개월 때 아이를 조산했다.
The woman gave birth prematurely when she was eight months pregnant.

그녀는 첫째 딸을 낳기 전에 한 번 유산했다.
She miscarried once before giving birth to her first daughter.

그 부부는 아이가 생기지 않아서 오랫동안 고생했다.
The couple suffered for a long time because they couldn't have a baby.

자연 임신을 시도하다
try to conceive
[get pregnant] naturally

인공수정을 하다
do artificial
insemination

시험관 시술(체외 수정)을 하다
do IVF(in vitro fertilization)

난자를 냉동하다
freeze one's eggs

정자 은행에서 받은 정자를 사용하다
use sperm from a sperm bank

대리모를 통해 아기를 낳다
give birth to a baby
through a surrogate mother

SENTENCES TO USE

우리는 인공 수정을 몇 번 시도한 후 시험관 시술을 통해 아이를 낳았다.
We tried artificial insemination a few times before giving birth to a baby
through in vitro fertilization.

젊었을 때 난자를 냉동해 두는 여성들이 늘고 있다.
More and more women freeze their eggs when they are young.

그 여성은 정자 은행에서 정자를 기증받아 아들을 낳았다.
The woman gave birth to a son with sperm from a sperm bank.

젖을[모유를] 먹이다
breastfeed
one's baby

분유를 먹이다
bottle-feed
one's baby

아기를 트림시키다
burp
one's baby

아기를 안다
hold
one's baby

아기를 등에 업다
carry one's baby
on one's back

아기를 유모차에 태우다
take one's baby in a stroller
[baby carriage,
pram, pushchair]

아기를 목욕시키다
give one's baby
a bath,
bathe one's baby

우는 아기를 달래다
soothe[calm]
a crying baby

보채는/칭얼대는
아기를 달래다
soothe one's upset/
whining baby

기저귀를 갈다
change
the diaper

아기를 침대에 누이다
lay one's baby
on the bed

아기를 재우다
put one's baby
to sleep

아기를 달래서
재우다
lull one's baby
to sleep

아기에게 자장가를
불러 주다
sing a lullaby
to one's baby

SENTENCES TO USE

나는 가능하면 아이에게 모유를 먹이고 싶다.　　　　I want to breastfeed my child if possible.

아기에게 모유를 먹이고 나면 트림을 시켜야 한다.
You should burp your baby after breastfeeding them.

그 남자는 아기를 등에 업었다.　　　　The man carried the baby on his back.

우는 아기를 달래는 일은 어렵다.　　　　It's hard to soothe a crying baby.

그 부부는 번갈아 가면서 아기를 재운다.
The couple take turns putting their baby to sleep.

육아를 전담하다
raise one's child
entirely alone

아기를 ~에게 맡기다
leave one's baby
with ~

육아 휴직을 하다
take maternity
[paternity] leave

육아 휴직 중이다
be on maternity
[paternity] leave

아기가 눈을 맞추다
make eye contact
(with ~)

이유식을 만들다
make baby food
[baby weaning food]

턱받이를 해 주다
put a bib
on one's baby

아기를 보행기에 태우다
put one's baby
in a baby walker

걸음마 훈련을 시키다
teach one's baby to walk,
help a baby learn to walk

대소변 가리는 훈련을 시키다
toilet train one's child,
potty-train one's child

숟가락/젓가락 쓰는 훈련을 시키다
teach one's baby to use
a spoon/chopsticks

SENTENCES TO USE

그녀는 낮에 아기를 친정어머니에게 맡기고 회사에 다닌다.
She leaves her baby with her mother during the day and goes to work.

요즘은 점점 더 많은 남성들이 육아 휴직을 하고 있다.
These days, more and more men are taking paternity leave.

생후 4주가 되면 아기가 눈을 맞추기 시작한다.
At four weeks of age, the baby begins to make eye contact.

그녀는 요즘 아기 이유식 만드는 재미에 빠졌다.
She is into making baby food these days.

저는 요즘 아이에게 대소변 가리는 훈련을 시키고 있어요.
I'm toilet training my child these days.

100일을 축하하다
celebrate one's
100th day

돌잔치를 하다
have[throw] a first
birthday party

양육 수당을 신청하다/받다
apply for/get
the childcare
allowance[child benefit]

아이에게 예방
접종을 시키다
get one's child
vaccinated

아이 건강 검진을 받게 하다
take the child to the
pediatrician for a
(regular) check-up

(아이가) 떼를 쓰다
have[throw]
a tantrum

~에게 책을 읽어 주다
read ~ a book,
read to ~

~에게 스마트폰/유튜브 영상/
TV를 보여 주다
show ~ smartphone/
YouTube videos/TV

~를 어린이집/유치원/
초등학교에 보내다
send ~ to daycare center/
kindergarten/elementary school

아이의 선생님과 상담하다
consult one's
child's teacher

~의 공부를 봐 주다
help ~ study 과목,
help ~ with
과목 studies

SENTENCES TO USE

우리 부부는 지난 토요일에 아이의 100일을 축하했다.
My wife and I celebrated our child's 100th day last Saturday.

내일은 아이에게 예방 접종을 시키러 간다.　　　I'm going to get my child vaccinated tomorrow.

그는 매일 밤 아이가 자기 전에 아이에게 책을 읽어 준다.
He reads to his child every night before he goes to bed.

많은 부모들이 아이들을 조용히 시키고 싶을 때는 아이들에게 스마트폰으로 유튜브 영상을 보여 준다.
Many parents show their children YouTube videos on their smartphones when they
want to keep them quiet.

그녀는 매일 퇴근 후에 딸아이의 영어와 수학 공부를 봐 준다.
She helps her daughter study English and math after work every day.

~에게 (…하는)
심부름을 시키다
send ~ on an errand (to 동사원형),
make ~ run an errand (to 동사원형)

~에게 집안일을 시키다
have[make] ~ do
housework[chores]

~에게 좋은 습관을 길러 주다
help ~ build[develop]
a good habit

~에게 다양한 경험을 쌓게 하다
have ~ experience many things

~를 칭찬하다
praise ~

~를 격려하다
encourage ~

~를 혼내다
scold ~

~를 말로 타이르다
reason with ~,
persuade ~

~에게 화를 내다
get angry with ~,
get mad at ~

~를 통제하다
control ~

SENTENCES TO USE

그녀는 아이에게 간장을 사 오라고 심부름을 시켰다. She sent her child on an errand to buy some soy sauce.

아이에게 집안일을 전혀 안 시키는 게 좋은 걸까요?
Is it good not to have your child do any housework?

아이들에게 좋은 습관을 길러 주려면 부모가 좋은 습관을 지녀야 한다.
Parents must have good habits to help their children develop good habits.

우리는 아이에게 다양한 경험을 쌓게 해 주려고 노력한다.
We try to have our child experience many things.

나는 아이들을 자주 칭찬하고 격려하는 게 좋다고 생각한다.
I think it's good to praise and encourage children often.

~에게 사교육을 시키다
send ~ to
a (private) lesson

~를 학원에 보내다
send ~ to
a private academy

~를 영어/수학/피아노/미술 학원에 보내다
send ~ to an English/a math/
a piano/an art lesson

~ 과외를 시키다
have a ~ tutor

~가 적성을 찾게 도와주다
help ~ find one's aptitude

~에게 적기 교육을 시키다
give ~ timely education

SENTENCES TO USE

한국 부모들은 자녀들에게 사교육을 많이 시킨다.
Korean parents send their children to many private lessons.

그녀는 아이를 영어, 수학, 피아노 학원에 보낸다.
She sends her child to English, math, and piano lessons.

부모는 아이가 적성을 찾도록 도와줘야 한다.
Parents should help their children find their aptitude.

아이들에게 필요한 것은 조기 교육이 아니라 적기 교육이다.
What children need is not early education, but timely education.

~를 현장 학습에 보내다
send ~ on a field trip

학부모 참관 수업에 참여하다
attend an open class
for parents

~를 전학시키다
transfer ~ to
another school

~를 (조기) 유학을 보내다
send ~ to study abroad
(at an early age)

~를 대안학교에 보내다
send ~ to an
alternative school

~가 지능 검사를 받게 하다
have ~ get an IQ test

육아책을 읽다
read books on parenting

SENTENCES TO USE

나는 오늘 딸아이 학교에서 학부모 참관 수업에 참여했다.
I attended an open class for parents at my daughter's school.

그는 아들이 중학교 때 유학을 보냈다.
He sent his son to study abroad when he was in middle school.

그 부모는 학교생활을 잘하지 못했던 아이를 대안학교에 보냈다.
The parents sent their child who had not done well at school to an alternative school.

그녀는 교육에 관심이 있어서 육아서 읽는 걸 좋아한다.
She likes reading books on parenting as she's interested in education.

여가, 취미

LEISURE & HOBBIES

(~로) 여행 가다
travel (to ~), take a trip (to ~),
go on a trip (to ~),
go on a journey (to ~)

여행 짐을 꾸리다
pack for one's journey,
pack one's bag
[suitcase, luggage]

(~로) 당일 여행을 가다
take a day trip (to ~),
go on a day trip (to ~)

~박 …일 여행을 가다
travel for ~ nights and
… days

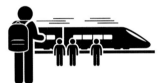

국내 여행을 하다
travel within one's
home country

해외여행을 하다
travel abroad

배낭여행을 가다
go backpacking,
go on a backpacking trip

패키지여행을 하다
go on a package
tour

크루즈 여행을 하다
go on a cruise

SENTENCES TO USE

팬데믹이 끝나면 나는 미국으로 여행을 가고 싶다.
When the pandemic is over, I want to travel to the United States.

우리 가족은 시골로 당일 여행을 자주 간다.
My family often goes on a day trip to the country.

나는 몇 년 전에 이탈리아로 여행 가서 7박 8일 동안 있었다.
A few years ago, I traveled to Italy and stayed for 7 nights and 8 days.

그녀는 20대 때 50일 동안 배낭여행을 했다.
She went backpacking for 50 days when she was in her 20s.

수학여행을 가다
go on
a school trip

졸업 여행을 가다
go on
a graduation trip

신혼여행을 가다
go on
a honeymoon

국토 횡단[종단] 여행을 하다
go on a cross-country trip

~ 답사를 가다
go on a field trip to explore ~

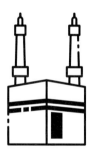

~로 성지 순례를 가다
go on[make]
a pilgrimage to ~

세계 일주를 하다
travel around
the world

SENTENCES TO USE

그들은 제주도로 졸업 여행을 갔다.
They went on a graduation trip to Jeju Island.

그녀는 대학교 때 국토 종단 여행을 했다.
She went on a cross-country trip when she was in college.

그들은 바티칸으로 성지 순례를 갔다.
They went on a pilgrimage to the Vatican.

그는 복권에 당첨되어서 세계 일주를 하기로 결심했다.
He won the lottery and decided to travel around the world.

여행 계획을 세우다
plan a trip,
make a tour plan

여행 경로를 정하다
set a route
for a trip

호텔방/호스텔/비앤비/
에어비앤비를 예약하다
book[reserve] a hotel room/
a hostel/a B&B/an Airbnb

(~행) 기차표/버스표/
비행기표를 구입하다
buy a train ticket/
a bus ticket/
a plane ticket
[a flight] (to ~)

(~행) 기차/버스/
비행기표를 예약하다
book a train ticket/a bus ticket/
a plane ticket[a flight] (to ~)

자동차/기차/버스/
비행기로 가다
go by car/train/
bus/plane

비행기/기차/버스로 ~를 여행하다
travel (to) ~
by plane/train/bus

비행기/기차/버스를 갈아타다
change planes/
trains/buses

SENTENCES TO USE

때로는 여행 계획을 세우는 것이 여행을 하는 것보다 더 설레기도 한다.
Sometimes planning a trip is more exciting than traveling.

그는 여름휴가를 위해 파리행 비행기표를 예약했다.
He booked a flight to Paris for his summer vacation.

우리는 자동차로 샌프란시스코에 갔다. We went to San Francisco by car.

그들은 코펜하겐에 가는 길에 런던에서 비행기를 갈아탔다.
They changed planes in London on their way to Copenhagen.

**호텔/호스텔/비앤비/
에어비앤비에 묵다**
stay at a hotel/a hostel/
a B&B/an Airbnb

~에 체크인하다
check in at ~

~에서 체크아웃하다
check out of ~

호텔 뷔페를 이용하다/호텔 뷔페에서 먹다
use a hotel buffet/
eat at a hotel buffet

관광 안내소에서 여행 정보를 문의하다
ask about travel information at
a tourist information center

렌터카를 빌리다
rent a car

고속도로 휴게소에 들르다
stop by[at] a highway
service[rest] area

고속도로 휴게소에서 식사를 하다
have a meal at a highway
service[rest] area

SENTENCES TO USE

나는 영국 웨일스에서 비앤비에 묵었다. I stayed at a B&B in Wales, in the UK.

그들은 기차역 근처에 있는 한 호텔에 체크인했다.
They checked in at a hotel near the train station.

그녀는 기차역에 있는 관광 안내소에서 몇 가지 여행 정보를 문의했다.
She asked about some travel information at the tourist information center
at the train station.

우리는 목적지로 가는 길에 고속도로 휴게소에서 가벼운 식사를 했다.
We had a light meal at the highway service area on the way to the destination.

관광 명소에 가다
go to[visit]
a tourist attraction

가이드 투어에 참여하다
take part in
[participate in]
a guided tour

쇼핑/관광을 즐기다
enjoy shopping/
sightseeing

맛집에 가다
go to a good[famous]
restaurant

맛집을 찾아보다
look for a
good[famous]
restaurant

맛집의 후기를 살펴보다
look at the reviews
of good[famous]
restaurants

~의 사진을 찍다
take pictures of ~

~에게 …의 사진을
찍어 달라고 부탁하다
ask ~ to take a picture of …

기념품을 사다
buy a souvenir

SENTENCES TO USE

나는 루브르 박물관에서 가이드 투어에 참여했다.
I participated in a guided tour at the Louvre Museum.

중국인 관광객들은 그 도시에서 쇼핑과 관광을 즐겼다.
The Chinese tourists enjoyed shopping and sightseeing in the city.

여행을 가면 반드시 맛집에 가는 사람들이 있다.
Some people always go to famous restaurants when they go on a trip.

그는 혼자 여행 중이어서 다른 여행객에게 자기 사진을 찍어 달라고 부탁했다.
He was traveling alone, so he asked another traveler to take a picture of him.

나는 여행을 가면 그곳을 기억하기 위한 작은 기념품을 산다.
When I go on a trip, I buy a small souvenir to remember that place.

공항 면세점에서 ~를 구입하다
buy ~
at the airport duty-free shop

보안 검색을 받다
get a security check
보안 검색을 통과하다
pass through security

공항 출입국 심사대를 통과하다
pass through the
immigration checkpoint

수하물 찾는 곳에서 짐을 찾다
pick up one's luggage
at the baggage claim area

세관을 통과하다
go[pass] through
customs

여행을 마치고 돌아오다
return[come back]
from one's trip
[travel, journey]

SNS/블로그에
여행 사진과 후기를 올리다
post photos[pictures] and reviews
of one's trip on one's SNS/blog

SENTENCES TO USE

여행에서 돌아오는 길에 공항 면세점에서 몇 가지 간식을 구입했다.
On my way back from my trip, I bought some snacks at the airport duty-free shop.

보안 검색을 통과하려면 모자와 신발을 벗어야 한다.
You have to take off your hat and shoes to pass through security.

입국 심사대를 통과한 후 수하물 찾는 곳에서 짐을 찾았다.
After passing through the immigration checkpoint, I picked up my luggage
at the baggage claim area.

여행에서 돌아오면 나는 블로그에 사진과 후기를 올린다.
After I come back from a trip, I post pictures and reviews on my blog.

2 TV, 유튜브, 넷플릭스

MP3 **064**

TV를 보다
watch TV

VOD로 TV 방송을 보다
watch TV shows through
VOD services

리모컨으로 채널을 바꾸다
change the TV channel
by a remote (control)

채널을 이리저리 돌리다
quickly scan through
different TV channels

IPTV에서 영화를 보다
watch a movie
on IPTV

유튜브 영상을 보다
watch a YouTube video,
watch a video on YouTube

유튜브 채널을 구독하다
subscribe to
a YouTube channel

**유튜브에서
라이브 방송을 보다**
watch a YouTube
live stream

**유튜브 영상에
'좋아요'를 누르다**
like a video on
YouTube

**유튜브 영상에
댓글을 달다**
post a comment on
a YouTube video

**유튜브 영상/음악을
다운로드하다**
download videos/
music from YouTube

SENTENCES TO USE

요즘은 VOD로 지난 TV 프로그램을 볼 수 있다.
Nowadays, you can watch old TV shows through VOD services.

극장에 가지 않아도 집에서 IPTV로 최신 영화를 볼 수 있다.
You can watch the latest movies on IPTV at home without going to the theater.

그는 매일 3시간 넘게 유튜브 영상을 본다.
He watches YouTube videos for more than three hours every day.

나는 한 영화평론가의 유튜브 채널을 구독하고 있다. I subscribe to a movie critic's YouTube channel.

유튜브 영상에 무례한 댓글을 다는 사람들이 있다.
There are people who post rude comments on YouTube videos.

유튜브 채널을
개설하다
open a
YouTube channel

유튜브에서
라이브
방송을 하다
live stream
on YouTube

유튜브에 올릴
영상을 촬영하다/제작하다
shoot/make a video to
upload to[on] YouTube

유튜브에 올릴
영상을 편집하다
edit a video to upload
to[on] YouTube

유튜브에 영상을
올리다
upload a video
to[on] YouTube

넷플릭스에 가입하다
subscribe to Netflix

넷플릭스를 보다
watch Netflix

넷플릭스에서 TV 프로그램/영화/다큐멘터리를 보다
watch a TV show/
a movie/a documentary on Netflix

넷플릭스를 해지하다
cancel one's Netflix subscription

SENTENCES TO USE

유튜브에 올릴 20분짜리 영상을 편집하는 데 8시간 정도가 걸린다.
It takes about eight hours to edit a 20-minute video to upload to YouTube.

그 유튜버는 자신의 유튜브 채널에 영상을 일주일에 2편씩 올린다.
The YouTuber uploads two videos a week on his YouTube channel.

나는 지난주에 넷플릭스에 가입했다.　　　　I subscribed to Netflix last week.

그녀는 넷플릭스에서 다큐멘터리를 보는 게 취미다.　Her hobby is watching documentaries on Netflix.

넷플릭스에 가입했지만 거의 보질 않아서 몇 달 후에 해지했다.
I subscribed to Netflix, but I barely watched it, so I canceled my subscription
after a few months.

MP3 065

축구/야구/농구/배구 경기를 보러 가다
go to see a soccer/baseball/
basketball/volleyball game

축구/야구/농구/배구 경기를 보다
watch a soccer/baseball/
basketball/volleyball game

축구/야구/농구/배구를 하다
play soccer/baseball/
basketball/volleyball

배드민턴/테니스/탁구/골프를 치다
play badminton/tennis/
table tennis[ping pong]/golf

조깅하러/수영하러/등산하러/
하이킹하러[등산하러]/스키 타러/스케이트 타러 가다
go jogging/swimming/mountain climbing/
hiking/skiing/skating

번지점프, 스카이다이빙 같은
익스트림 스포츠를 즐기다
enjoy extreme sports
such as bunjee jumping
and sky diving

마라톤을 하다
run a marathon

SENTENCES TO USE

나는 초등학교 때 아버지와 함께 처음 야구 경기를 보러 갔다.
I went to see a baseball game with my father for the first time when I was
in elementary school.

그는 주말마다 친구들과 농구를 한다.
He plays basketball with his friends every weekend.

우리 어머니는 매일 아침 수영하러 가신다. My mother goes swimming every morning.

나는 겨울에 자주 친구들하고 스케이트를 타러 다녔다.
I often went skating with my friends in winter.

그 소설가는 자주 마라톤을 한다. The novelist often runs marathons.

준비 운동을 하다
warm up,
do warm-up exercise(s)

유산소운동을 하다
do
aerobic exercise(s)

근력 운동을 하다
do
weight training

요가/필라테스를 하다
do[practice]
yoga/Pilates

체육관[헬스클럽]에 가다
go to the gym

PT를 받다
train with
a personal trainer

러닝머신에서 뛰다
run on a treadmill

스쿼트를 하다
do squats

플랭크를 하다
do planks

아령을/역기를
들어 올리다
lift a dumbbell/weights

윗몸일으키기를 하다
do sit-ups

파워 워킹을 하다
power walk

SENTENCES TO USE

운동하기 전에는 준비 운동을 하는 게 안전하다.　　It is safe to warm up before exercising.

살을 빼려면 식이 조절을 하고 유산소운동을 해야 한다.
To lose weight, you need to control your diet and do aerobic exercises.

요즘 많은 여성들이 필라테스를 한다.　　Many women do Pilates these days.

그녀는 헬스클럽에 가서 PT를 받는다.
She goes to the gym and trains with a personal trainer.

나는 매일 집에서 플랭크와 스쿼트를 한다.　　I do planks and squats at home every day.

등산을 가다
go hiking,
go mountain climbing

암벽 등반을 하다
go rock climbing

등산용품을 구입하다
buy hiking supplies

등산 동호회(산악회)에 가입하다
join a climbing club

등산화/등산복/등산모를 신다/입다/쓰다
wear hiking boots/
hiking clothes/an alpine hat

등산화 끈을 단단히 묶다
tie one's hiking boot
shoelaces tightly

야간 등산을 하다
go hiking at night

배낭을 메다
carry a backpack

SENTENCES TO USE

많은 이들이 주말에 등산을 다닌다.　　Many people go hiking on weekends.

그녀는 30대 때 암벽 등반을 자주 다녔다.
She often went rock climbing in her thirties.

그는 등산을 시작하고자 등산용품과 등산복, 등산화를 먼저 구입했다.
In order to start mountain climbing, he first bought hiking supplies, hiking clothes,
and hiking boots.

나는 야간 등산을 한 번 해 본 적이 있다.　　I've gone hiking at night once.

야호라고 외치다
shout hooray[hurray]

등산로를 따라가다
follow
a hiking trail

산에서 길을 잃다
get lost
in the mountains

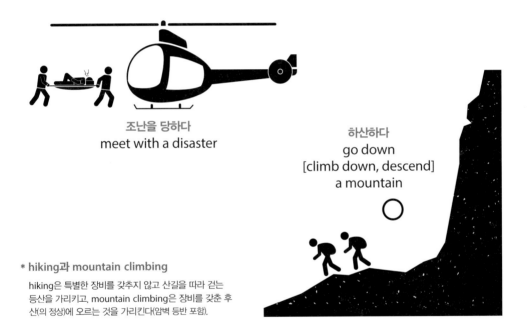

조난을 당하다
meet with a disaster

하산하다
go down
[climb down, descend]
a mountain

* hiking과 mountain climbing

hiking은 특별한 장비를 갖추지 않고 산길을 따라 걷는
등산을 가리키고, mountain climbing은 장비를 갖춘 후
산(의 정상)에 오르는 것을 가리킨다(암벽 등반 포함).

SENTENCES TO USE

그들은 산 정상에 올라서 야호라고 외쳤다.
They climbed to the top of the mountain and shouted "hooray".

산에서 길을 잃으면 어떻게 해야 할까?
What should you do if you get lost in the mountains?

그 등반가는 에베레스트산에서 하산하던 중에 조난을 당했다.
The climber met with a disaster while climbing down Mount Everest.

곧 해가 질 것 같아서 우리는 하산했다.
We went down the mountain because the sun was about to set.

UNIT 4

캠핑을 가다
go camping

캠핑카를 렌트하다/
구입하다
rent/buy a camper van
[camping car]

승합차를 개조해 캠핑카로 만들다
remodel a van
into a camper van
[camping car]

텐트를 치다/걷다
pitch[set up]/
take down a tent

텐트 안으로 들어가다
enter[go into] the tent

텐트 밖으로 나오다
come[step] out of the tent

차양을 치다
put up
an awning

모닥불을 피우다
make
a bonfire

바비큐를 해 먹다
have a barbecue,
enjoy a barbecue

침낭에서 자다
sleep in
a[one's]
sleeping bag

침낭을 펴다/말다
unroll/roll up
one's[the]
sleeping bag

모기장을 치다/걷다
put up[set up]/
take down
a mosquito net

차박을 하러 가다
go car camping

SENTENCES TO USE

요즘 점점 더 많은 사람들이 캠핑을 간다.　　　More and more people go camping these days.

그들은 승합차를 개조해서 캠핑카로 만들어 그걸 타고 캠핑을 다닌다.
They remodeled the van into a camper van and go camping in it.

우리는 캠핑장에 도착하여 우선 텐트를 쳤다.　　　We arrived at the camping site and pitched a tent first.

캠핑을 가면 우리는 으레 바비큐를 해 먹는다.　　　When we go camping, we usually have a barbecue.

우리는 텐트 속에 모기장을 치고 침낭에서 잤다.
We put up a mosquito net in the tent and slept in a sleeping bag.

MP3 067

호캉스를 하다
be on a staycation
at a hotel

호캉스를 가다
go on a staycation
at a hotel

호텔에 체크인하다
check in at a hotel

호텔에서 체크아웃하다
check out of a hotel

호텔 바에서 칵테일을 마시다
drink a cocktail at a hotel bar

(~로) 룸서비스를 시키다
order room service (for ~)

호텔 피트니스 센터를 이용하다
use the fitness center in a hotel

호텔 수영장에서 수영하다
swim in the hotel pool

SENTENCES TO USE

지난 주말에 우리는 호텔에서 1박 2일간 호캉스를 했다.
Last weekend, we were on a staycation at a hotel for 2 days and 1 night.

점점 더 많은 사람들이 호캉스를 하러 간다.
More and more people go on a staycation at hotels.

우리는 저녁으로 룸서비스를 시켰다.
We ordered room service for dinner.

우리는 호텔 수영장에서 수영을 하고 스파를 즐겼다.
We swam in the hotel pool and enjoyed the spa.

스파를 즐기다
enjoy the spa

건식/습식 사우나를 즐기다
enjoy the dry/wet sauna

도시의 야경을 감상하다
enjoy the night view
of the city

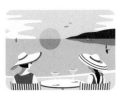

오션뷰를 감상하다
enjoy
the ocean view

마사지를 받다
get a massage

욕조에서 반신욕을 하다
take a lower-body bath
in the bathtub

조식 뷔페를 먹다
have a buffet breakfast

SENTENCES TO USE

도심에 있는 호텔이어서 우리는 도시의 야경을 감상할 수 있었다.
It was a hotel in the city center, so we could enjoy the night view of the city.

나는 호텔에서 발 마사지를 받았다.　　　　　　I got a foot massage at the hotel.

우리는 반신욕을 하고 잠자리에 들었다.
We took lower-body baths and went to bed.

그들은 조식 뷔페를 먹은 다음 체크아웃했다.
They had a buffet breakfast and then checked out.

해수욕을 가다
go swimming
in the sea[ocean]

(비치)파라솔을 빌리다
borrow a beach umbrella,
borrow a parasol

해수욕을 하다
(바다에서 수영을 하다)
swim in the sea

백사장에서 놀다
play on
the sandy beach

백사장에 눕다
lie on
the sandy beach

모래찜질을 하다
take a sand bath

선탠을 하다
get a tan

서핑을 하다
surf

스쿠버 다이빙을 하다
scuba dive

샤워를 해 소금기를 씻어내다
take a shower
to wash off the salt

SENTENCES TO USE

나는 어렸을 때 여름방학마다 부모님과 해수욕을 갔다.
When I was young, I went swimming in the sea with my parents every summer vacation.

우리는 해수욕장에 가면 우선 비치파라솔을 빌린다.
When we go to the beach, we borrow a beach umbrella first.

해변에 가도 나는 바다에서 수영을 하지는 않고 대신 백사장에서 놀았다.
Even if I went to the beach, I didn't swim in the sea but instead I played on the sandy beach.

백사장에서는 사람들이 선탠을 하거나 모래찜질을 하고 있었다.
On the sandy beach, people were getting a tan or taking a sand bath.

동해에는 서핑을 하는 사람들이 많이 있다.　　　There are a lot of people surfing in the East Sea.

영화표를 예매하다
book a movie ticket,
buy a movie ticket in advance
연극표/뮤지컬표를 예매하다
book a ticket for a play/musical

온라인으로 영화를 예매하다
book[reserve] a movie ticket online

영화를/연극을/뮤지컬을 보러 가다
go to see a movie/play/musical
영화를/연극을/뮤지컬을 보다
watch a movie/play/musical

영화가 개봉되다/영화를 개봉하다
a movie is released/release a movie
극장에서 영화를 보다
watch a movie in the theater
조조 영화를 보다
watch a matinee (movie)
심야 영화를 보다
watch a late-night movie

SENTENCES TO USE

나는 뮤지컬을 보는 게 가장 큰 취미이다.
My biggest hobby is watching musicals.

기다리던 영화가 개봉해서 온라인으로 예매했다.
The movie I was waiting for was released, and I booked tickets online.

그녀는 TV가 아니라 극장에서 영화 보는 것을 좋아한다.
She likes to watch movies at the theater, not on TV.

조조 영화를 보면 할인을 받을 수 있다.
You can get a discount if you watch a matinee.

IPTV로/넷플릭스로 영화를 보다
watch a movie on
IPTV/Netflix

드라이브인 극장에서 영화를 보다
watch a movie at
a drive-in theater

영화 시사회에 초대받다
be invited to a movie premiere

영화 시사회에 참석하다
attend a movie premiere

영화제에 가다
go to a film festival

SENTENCES TO USE

요즘은 극장뿐 아니라 IPTV나 넷플릭스로도 영화를 볼 수 있다.
Nowadays, we can watch movies not only in theaters but also on IPTV or Netflix.

드라이브인 극장에서 영화를 본 적 있어요?
Have you ever watched a movie at a drive-in theater?

나는 그 감독의 신작 영화 시사회에 초대받았다.
I was invited to the premiere of the director's new film.

그녀는 해마다 가을이면 부산국제영화제에 간다.
She goes to the Busan International Film Festival every fall.

극장에 입장하다
enter
a theater

입구에서 표를 확인받다
have[get] one's ticket
checked at the entrance

자리에 앉다
take a seat

휴대폰을 진동/무음 모드로 하다
put one's mobile phone on
vibrate/silent mode

영화 상영 전 광고를 보다
watch commercials
before the movie starts

엔딩 크레딧을 끝까지 보다
watch all the way to
the end of the credits

휴대폰을 끄다
turn off one's
mobile phone

영화를 보며 팝콘을 먹다/음료를 마시다
eat popcorn/have a soft drink
while watching a movie

~에게
큰 박수를
보내다
give ~
a big hand

커튼콜을 외치다
call the actors and actresses
before the curtain,
clap for a curtain call
(박수로 커튼콜에 불러내다)

박수 치다
clap, applaud

~에게 기립 박수를 보내다
give ~ a standing
ovation

SENTENCES TO USE

극장에 입장하면 휴대폰을 무음 모드로 하거나 꺼야 한다.
When you enter the theater, you must put your mobile phone on silent mode or turn it off.

팝콘을 먹는 소리가 가끔 영화 감상을 방해할 때가 있다.
The sound of eating popcorn sometimes interferes with watching movies.

나는 영화의 엔딩 크레딧을 끝까지 본다.　　　I watch all the way to the end of the credits.

관객들이 배우들에게 기립 박수를 보냈다.　　　The audience gave the actors a standing ovation.

연극이 끝나고 관객들이 박수로 커튼콜을 외쳤다.
After the play was over, the audience clapped for a curtain call.

7 음악, 콘서트

MP3 069

음악을 듣다
listen to music

노래를 스트리밍하다
stream
a song

노래를 다운로드하다
download
a song

콘서트[연주회] 표를
예매하다
book[reserve]
a concert ticket

콘서트[연주회]에 가다
go to a concert

환호하다
cheer, shout with joy

~에게 기립 박수를 보내다
give ~ a standing ovation

(~의) 노래를
따라 부르다
sing along
(with ~)

앙코르를 청하다
call for
an encore

악기/피아노/기타를 연주하다
play a musical
instrument/the piano/
the guitar

악기/피아노/기타 연주법을 배우다
learn to play a musical
instrument/the piano/
the guitar

SENTENCES TO USE

저는 그 노래의 MP3 파일을 다운로드받아서 자주 들어요.
I downloaded the MP3 file of the song and listen to it often.

예전에는 콘서트에 자주 갔는데 요즘은 통 못 간다.
I used to go to concerts often, but these days I can't.

청중이 박수를 치면서 뮤지션의 노래를 따라 부르고 있다.
The audience is clapping and singing along with the musician.

나는 예전부터 늘 드럼을 배우고 싶었다.
I've always wanted to learn to play drums.

(~의) 그림을 그리다
draw[paint]
a picture (of ~)

풍경화/정물화를 그리다
paint
a landscape/a still life

~의 초상화를 그리다
draw[paint]
a portrait of ~

(~의) 캐리커처를 그리다
draw a caricature (of ~)

수채화를 그리다
paint with[in] watercolors, paint a watercolor painting

유화를 그리다
paint in oils, paint an oil painting

컬러링북에 색칠하다
color in a coloring book

미술 전시회에 가다
go to an art exhibition

**전시품/작품/그림/
조각품을 감상하다**
enjoy[appreciate]
exhibits/works/
paintings/sculptures

**도슨트(안내인)의 설명을
들으며 작품을 감상하다**
appreciate[enjoy] works
listening to a docent's
explanation

카탈로그를/기념품을 구입하다
buy a catalogue/a souvenir

전시회 관람 예약을 하다
book[reserve] an exhibition ticket

SENTENCES TO USE

그녀는 어려서부터 그림 그리는 걸 좋아한다.
She has been fond of drawing pictures since she was a child.

그는 가끔 야외에 나가서 풍경화를 그린다.　　He sometimes goes outdoors and paints landscapes.

나는 좋아하는 소설가의 초상화를 그려서 선물했다.
I drew a portrait of my favorite novelist and presented it to him.

나는 요즘 캐리커처를 그리는 연습을 하고 있다.　　I'm practicing drawing caricatures these days.

그 뮤지션은 자주 미술 전시회에 가서 작품을 감상한다.
The musician often goes to art exhibitions and appreciates the works of art.

혹백 사진을 찍다
take a black-and-white photo[picture]
필름 카메라로 사진을 찍다
take a photo[picture] with a film camera
전문가용 카메라를 구입하다
buy a professional camera

사진을 찍다
take a photo,
take a picture

출사를 나가다
go out to take
photos[pictures]

초점을 잡다
get into
focus

셔터 스피드를 조정하다
adjust the
shutter speed

사진의 구도를 잡다
compose
a photo

삼각대에 카메라를 올리다
put a camera
on a tripod

모델/제품 촬영을 하다
shoot a model/
a product

셀카를 찍다
take a selfie

**셀카봉을 이용해
셀카를 찍다**
take a selfie using
a selfie stick

사진을 보정하다
retouch
[photoshop]
a photo

사진을 편집하다
edit a photo

사진을 인화하다
print a photo

SENTENCES TO USE

나는 우리 고양이 사진을 즐겨 찍는다.　　　　I enjoy taking pictures of my cat.

그녀는 오늘 단풍이 아름다운 계곡으로 출사를 나갔다.
She went out to take pictures of a valley with beautiful autumn leaves today.

너는 사진 구도 잡는 방법을 좀 배워야 해.　　　You need to learn how to compose a photo.

나는 셀카 찍는 걸 좋아하지 않는다.　　　　　I don't like taking selfies.

그녀가 인스타그램에 올리는 사진들은 보정을 많이 한 것들이다.
The photos she posts on Instagram are heavily retouched.

MP3 071

반려동물/개[강아지]/고양이를 입양하다
adopt a pet/dog[puppy]/cat

유기견을/유기묘를 입양하다
adopt an abandoned dog/cat

반려동물/개[강아지]/고양이를 키우다
have[raise] a pet/
dog[puppy]/cat

개/고양이에게 밥을
[사료를] 주다
feed one's dog/cat

반려동물에게 줄
간식을 만들다
make treats
for one's pet

반려동물에게
간식을 주다
give one's
pet treats

반려동물과 놀다
play with
one's pet

반려동물 용품을
구입하다
buy pet
supplies

반려동물을
동물병원에 데리고 가다
take one's pet to
an animal hospital

반려동물에게
예방접종을 시키다
get one's pet
vaccinated

반려동물을
등록하다
register
one's pet

반려동물에게
인식칩을 심다
microchip
one's pet

개를 산책시키다
walk one's
dog

개의
목줄[가슴줄]을 하다
put one's dog
on a leash

SENTENCES TO USE

그녀는 유기견을 입양했다.　　　　　　　She adopted an abandoned dog.

개와 고양이에게 사료는 정해진 시간에 주는 게 좋다.
You should feed your dogs and cats at a fixed time.

그녀는 자기 개에게 줄 간식을 직접 만든다.　　She makes treats for her dog herself.

나는 오늘 내 고양이를 동물병원에 데리고 갔다.　I took my cat to the animal hospital today.

개를 산책시킬 때는 반드시 목줄을 하고, 대변 처리를 깨끗이 해야 한다.
When you walk your dog, you must put it on a leash and clean up after it.

개에게 사회화
훈련을 시키다
socialize
one's dog

개/고양이
양치질을 시키다
brush one's
dog's/cat's teeth

개에게 입마개를
씌우다
muzzle
one's dog

(개가)
입마개를 하다
wear
a muzzle

강아지에게
대소변 가리는
훈련을 시키다
housebreak
a puppy

개의 대변을
처리하다
clean up after
one's dog

개/고양이를
목욕시키다
give one's
dog/cat a bath

개/고양이
미용을 시키다
get a haircut for
one's dog/cat

캣타워를 조립하다/만들다
assemble/build
a cat tree
[cat tower]

고양이의 숨숨집을
사다/만들다
buy/make
a cat house

고양이 화장실
모래를(배설물을) 치우다
clean
the cat litter

고양이 화장실 모래를 갈다
change the cat litter

고양이 화장실을 닦다
clean the
cat litter box

반려동물의 장례식을
치러 주다
hold a funeral
for one's pet

반려동물을
안락사시키다
have one's pet
put down

SENTENCES TO USE

맹견들은 산책할 때 입마개를 해야 한다.
Aggressive dogs should wear a muzzle when on a walk.

강아지 대소변 가리는 훈련을 시키는 건 쉽지 않다.   It is not easy to housebreak a puppy.

나는 DIY 캣타워를 사다가 직접 만들었다.   I bought a DIY cat tree and built it myself.

고양이 화장실 배설물은 매일 치워야 한다.
You must clean the cat litter every day.

고양이 화장실 모래는 얼마나 자주 갈아 줘야 하나요?
How often should I change the cat litter?

CHAPTER

6

스마트폰, 인터넷, 소셜 미디어

SMARTPHONE, THE INTERNET, SNS

1

전화, 스마트폰

전화를 걸다
make a (phone) call

전화를 받다
answer[get] a (phone) call,
answer the phone

통화하다
talk on
the phone

영상통화를 하다
make[do]
a video call

문자를 보내다
text, send a text
message

사진/동영상을 보내다
send a photo
[picture]/video

메신저앱으로 대화하다
talk on
a messenger app

스마트폰을 잠그다
lock one's
smartphone

스마트폰 잠금을 풀다
unlock one's
smartphone

밀어서 스마트폰의 잠금을 풀다
slide to unlock one's smartphone,
unlock one's smartphone by
sliding to the right

SENTENCES TO USE

나는 설거지를 하느라 전화를 받지 못했다.
I couldn't answer the phone because I was washing the dishes.

지구 반대편에 있는 사람들끼리도 영상통화를 하며 얼굴을 보고 대화할 수 있다.
People on opposite sides of the world can make video calls and talk face to face.

운전 중에 문자를 보내는 건 위험하다.   It's dangerous to text while driving.

메신저앱으로 대화하는 게 통화하는 것보다 편하다는 사람들이 있다.
Some people say that talking on messenger apps is more comfortable than talking
on the phone.

그 사람의 스마트폰은 잠겨 있지 않았다.   His smartphone was not locked.

비밀번호를/패턴을 입력하여 스마트폰의 잠금을 풀다
enter a password/pattern to unlock one's
smartphone, unlock one's smartphone
by entering a password/pattern

지문을 인식하여 스마트폰의 잠금을 풀다
unlock one's smartphone
with a fingerprint

스마트폰으로 인터넷에 접속하다
access the Internet with one's
smartphone, use one's smartphone
to access the Internet[to get online]

스마트폰으로 인터넷을 이용하다
use the Internet with one's
smartphone

앱을 사용하다
use an
application[app]

앱을 검색하다
search for an
application[app]

앱을 다운로드하다
download
an application
[app]

앱을 깔다[설치하다]
install
an application
[app]

앱을 업데이트하다
update
an application
[app]

앱을 삭제하다
delete
an application
[app]

SENTENCES TO USE

나는 패턴을 입력하여 내 스마트폰의 잠금을 푼다.   I unlock my smartphone by entering a pattern.

요즘은 대부분의 사람들이 스마트폰으로 인터넷에 접속한다.
Nowadays, most people access the Internet with their smartphones.

나는 운동을 관리해 주는 앱을 사용하고 있다.   I'm using an app that tracks my workouts.

그녀는 지역 도서관 앱을 다운로드하여 설치했다.   She downloaded and installed the local library app.

나는 사용하지 않는 앱을 여러 개 삭제했다.   I deleted several apps that I didn't use.

모바일 뱅킹을 하다
use mobile banking

스마트폰을 TV에 미러링하다
(스마트폰 화면을 TV로 보다)
mirror[cast] one's smartphone
screen to a TV

스마트폰의 배경화면을 바꾸다
change the wallpaper of
a smartphone

스마트폰의 설정을 바꾸다
change the settings
on one's smartphone

스마트폰을 진동 모드로/
무음 모드로 바꾸다
put one's smartphone on vibrate/silent mode

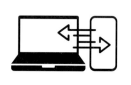

스마트폰을 PC와 동기화하다
synchronize one's
smartphone with a PC

와이파이를 검색하다
search for a Wi-Fi
network

전화기를 충전하다
charge one's phone

전화기를 고속 충전하다
fast charge one's phone

SENTENCES TO USE

모바일 뱅킹을 사용하면 언제 어디서나 송금을 할 수 있다.
If you use mobile banking, you can transfer money anytime, anywhere.

스마트폰을 TV에 미러링해서 TV로 유튜브를 볼 수 있다.
You can watch YouTube on TV by mirroring your smartphone screen to a TV.

그녀는 스마트폰 배경화면을 매일 바꾼다.   She changes her smartphone wallpaper every day.

우리는 와이파이를 검색해서 무료 와이파이에 접속했다.
We searched for a Wi-Fi network and connected to a free one.

배터리가 거의 떨어져서 전화기를 충전해야 한다.
The battery is almost dead, so I have to charge my phone.

2 인터넷, 이메일

MP3 073

인터넷을 깔다[설치하다]
set up a modem,
set up a network

인터넷에 접속하다
connect to the
Internet

무선 인터넷을 이용하다
use wireless
Internet

네트워크 연결이 끊어지다
the network
is down

웹사이트에 접속하다
access a website

인터넷을 서핑하다
surf[browse] the
Internet

포털 사이트에서 정보를 검색하다
search[look] for information on
a portal site

구글로 검색하다
google (동사)

웹사이트에 가입하다
sign up for a
website

웹사이트에서 탈퇴하다
delete one's account from a website,
close one's account at a website

SENTENCES TO USE

요즘은 대부분 무선 인터넷을 쓴다.
Nowadays, most people use wireless Internet.

가끔 인터넷을 하다 보면 네트워크 연결이 끊어진다.
Sometimes when I use the Internet, the network is down.

그녀는 틈만 나면 인터넷 서핑을 한다.
She surfs the Internet whenever she has time.

요즘 사람들은 보통 포털 사이트에서 정보나 뉴스를 검색한다.
Nowadays, people usually search for information or news on portal sites.

나는 궁금한 게 생기면 바로 구글로 검색한다.
When I want to know something, I google it right away.

웹사이트에 로그인하다
log in[on] to
a website

웹사이트에서 로그아웃하다
log out of
a website

ID와 비밀번호를 입력하다
enter one's user ID
and password

웹사이트를 즐겨찾기 하다
bookmark a website,
put a website on one's
favorites list

인터넷[온라인]
쇼핑을 하다
shop online

인터넷 뱅킹을 사용하다
use Internet
banking

인터넷 게임을 하다
play an Internet[online]
game

웹사이트를 해킹하다
hack into a website

파일을 공유하다
share a file

복사하다
copy

붙여 넣다
paste

SENTENCES TO USE

비밀번호를 잊어버려서 그 웹사이트에 로그인하지 못했다.
I couldn't log in to the website because I forgot my password.

나는 그 웹사이트를 즐겨찾기 해 두었다.　　　　I've bookmarked that website.

요즘 사람들은 채소를 포함한 대부분의 물건을 온라인에서 쇼핑한다.
Nowadays, people shop online for most things, including vegetables.

그는 휴가 때는 새벽까지 인터넷 게임을 한다.
He plays Internet games until dawn when he's on vacation.

한 중학생이 그 신문사의 웹사이트를 해킹했다.
A middle school student hacked into the newspaper's website.

이메일 계정을 만들다
create an email account

이메일 계정에 로그인하다
log in[on] to one's email account

이메일 계정에서 로그아웃하다
log out of one's email account

회사에서 이메일 계정을 받다
get an email account from one's company

이메일을 쓰다
write an email

이메일을 보내다
send an email

이메일을 자신에게 보내다
send an email to oneself

이메일에
파일을 첨부하다
attach a file to
an email

이메일에 답장하다
reply to an email

이메일을 전달하다
forward
an email

참조로 ~에게 이메일을 보내다
CC(carbon copy) an email to
someone, CC someone on an
email, copy someone on an email

숨은 참조로 ~에게 이메일을 보내다
BCC(blind carbon copy)
an email to someone,
BCC someone on an email

SENTENCES TO USE

나는 그 이메일 계정에 하루에 한 번 로그인한다.　　I log in to that email account once a day.

요즘은 업무 외에는 이메일을 쓰는 일이 별로 없다.
These days, I don't usually write emails except for work.

그녀는 이메일에 그 파일을 첨부해서 보냈다.　　She attached the file to the email.

나는 오늘 밀린 이메일 몇 통에 답장을 보냈다.　　Today I replied to a few overdue emails.

그는 그 메일을 팀장에게 참조로 보냈다.　　He CC'd his manager on the email.

이메일을 임시 저장하다
save an email
temporarily

이메일을 미리 보기하다
preview
an email

이메일을 삭제하다
delete an email

스팸메일을 영구 삭제하다
permanently delete
a spam[junk] email

이메일을 백업하다
save a copy of
an email

이메일을 스팸 처리하다
mark an email
as spam

휴지통을 비우다
empty the trash can

이메일 계정 환경을 설정하다
set up
email preferences

이메일 계정을 삭제하다
delete an email account

이메일 계정이 휴면 계정으로 바뀌다
one's email account becomes dormant[inactive]

SENTENCES TO USE

나는 이메일을 보내기 전에 미리 보기를 한다.	I preview an email before I send it.
불필요한 이메일은 삭제하는 게 좋다.	You should delete unnecessary emails.
나는 광고성 이메일은 스팸 처리한다.	I mark email ads as spam.
메일함의 휴지통은 자주 비우세요.	Empty the trash can in your email box often.
나는 쓰지 않는 이메일 계정을 삭제했다.	I deleted the email account I wasn't using.

블로그를 운영하다
have[run] a blog

블로그에 게시물을 올리다
write[put] a post on one's blog

트위터/인스타그램/페이스북에 가입하다
join Twitter/Instagram/Facebook

트위터/인스타그램/페이스북 계정을 만들다
create a Twitter/an Instagram/a Facebook account

트위터/인스타그램/페이스북 계정이 있다
have a Twitter/an Instagram/a Facebook account

트위터/인스타그램/페이스북을 이용하다
use Twitter/Instagram/Facebook

트윗하다
tweet

트위터/인스타그램/페이스북에 ~를 올리다
post ~ on Twitter/Instagram/Facebook

트위터/인스타그램/페이스북에서 ~를 팔로우하다
follow ~ on Twitter/Instagram/Facebook

DM을 보내다/받다
send/receive a DM(direct message)

~에 악플을 달다
post hateful comments on ~

SENTENCES TO USE

그녀는 요리 블로그를 운영한다.   She runs a cooking blog.

나는 최근에 인스타그램에 가입했다.   I recently joined Instagram.

나는 페이스북 계정을 만들었다가 금방 없앴다.   I created a Facebook account but I quickly deleted it.

나는 트윗을 올리지는 않고 다른 사람들의 트윗만 본다.
I don't tweet; instead I just look at other people's tweets.

다른 사람들의 SNS에 악플을 다는 사람들이 생각보다 많다.
More people post hateful comments on other people's SNS than I thought.

유튜브 채널을
개설하다
open a
YouTube channel

유튜브에 올릴 영상을
촬영하다/제작하다
shoot/make a video to
upload to[on] YouTube

유튜브에 올릴
영상을 편집하다
edit a video to upload
to[on] YouTube

유튜브에 영상을
올리다
upload a video
to[on] YouTube

유튜브에서 라이브 방송을 하다
live stream
on YouTube

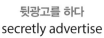

앞광고를 하다
openly advertise

뒷광고를 하다
secretly advertise

조회수가 ~회를 돌파하다
have more than
~ views

구독자가 10만 명/100만 명이 되다
have a hundred thousand/
one million subscribers

실버 버튼/골드 버튼을 받다
get[receive] a Silver/Gold Play Button

실버 버튼/골드 버튼 언박싱을 하다
unbox a Silver/Gold Play Button

댓글을 (맨 위에) 고정하다
pin a YouTube comment to the top,
put a YouTube comment at the top

SENTENCES TO USE

그 여행 작가는 유튜브 채널을 개설했다.
The travel writer opened a YouTube channel.

그녀는 자신의 유튜브 채널에 영상을 매일 올린다.
She uploads videos to her YouTube channel every day.

그 가수는 일주일에 한 번씩 유튜브 라이브 방송을 한다.
The singer live streams on YouTube once a week.

누군가 고양이를 목욕시키는 그 영상은 조회수가 400만이 넘는다.
The YouTube video of someone giving a cat a bath has more than 4 million views.

그 유튜브 채널은 구독자가 10만 명을 넘어서 실버 버튼을 받았다.
The YouTube channel received a Silver Play Button with over 100,000 subscribers.

유튜브 채널을 구독하다
subscribe to
a YouTube channel

유튜브 영상을 보다
watch a YouTube video, watch a video on YouTube
1.25/1.5배속으로 유튜브 영상을 보다
watch a YouTube video at 1.25x/1.5x speed

유튜브
라이브 방송을 보다
watch a YouTube
live stream

유튜브에서 광고를
건너뛰다
skip ads
on YouTube

유튜브 영상에
'좋아요'를 누르다
like a video on
YouTube

유튜브 영상에 댓글을 달다
write a comment on
a YouTube video

유튜브 음악을/영상을
다운로드하다
download music/
videos from
YouTube

유튜브에서 음원을
추출하다
extract audio from
a YouTube video

유튜브 영상을
~와 공유하다
share
a YouTube
video with ~

유튜브/트위터/인스타그램/
페이스북에서 ~를 차단하다
block someone on
YouTube/Twitter/
Instagram/Facebook

SENTENCES TO USE

나는 30개가 넘는 유튜브 채널을 구독한다.　　I subscribe to over 30 YouTube channels.

그 사람은 말을 느리게 해서 나는 그 사람 유튜브 영상은 1.25배속으로 본다.
He talks slowly, so I watch his YouTube videos at 1.25x speed.

그는 유튜브 라이브 방송을 자주 본다.　　He often watches YouTube live streams.

나는 그 유튜버의 영상을 볼 때는 광고를 건너뛰지 않는다.
I don't skip ads when I watch that YouTuber's videos.

나는 유튜브 동영상을 보면 항상 '좋아요'를 누른다.　When I watch a YouTube video, I always "like" it.

나는 재미있는 유튜브 영상을 가끔 친구들에게 공유한다.
I sometimes share interesting YouTube videos with my friends.

CHAPTER

7

대중교통, 운전

PUBLIC TRANSPORTATION & DRIVING

버스, 지하철, 택시, 기차

MP3 **075**

버스/지하철/택시/기차/
고속버스를 타다
take a bus/a subway/a taxi/
a train/an express bus

버스/지하철/택시/기차/
고속버스로 ~에 가다
go to ~ by bus/subway/
taxi/train/express bus

버스/지하철에 오르다
get on a bus/
the subway

버스/지하철에서 내리다
get off a bus/
the subway

택시를 타다, 택시에 오르다
get in a taxi
택시에서 내리다
get out of a taxi

버스/열차를 잡다
catch a bus/train

버스/열차를 놓치다
miss a bus/train

교통카드를 충전하다
charge one's
transportation card

일회용 교통카드를 구입하다
buy a single journey ticket

일회용 교통카드 보증금을 환급받다
get a refund on the[one's]
single journey ticket deposit

2층 버스를 타다
take a
double-decker (bus)

SENTENCES TO USE

그녀는 택시를 타고 병원에 진료를 보러 갔다.
She took a taxi to go see a doctor.

버스에 오를 때 전화벨이 울렸다.
The phone rang as I got on the bus.

택시에서 내리는데 빗방울이 떨어지기 시작했다.
As I got out of the taxi, raindrops began to fall.

나는 8시 열차를 놓쳐서 회사에 지각했다.
I was late for work because I missed the 8 o'clock train.

오늘 출근길에 교통카드를 충전해야 한다.
I have to charge my transportation card on my way to work today.

내리면 일회용 교통카드 보증금을 환급받으세요.
Get a refund on your single journey ticket deposit when you get off.

버스/지하철
시간표를 확인하다
check the bus/subway
timetable[schedule]

버스/지하철 노선도를 확인하다
check the bus/subway (route) map
내려야 할 버스 정거장/지하철역을 확인하다
check the bus stop/subway station to get off

지하철 개찰구를 통과하다
go through the
subway turnstile

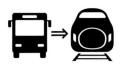

A에서 B로
환승하다
transfer from
A to B

버스/지하철에서
자리를 잡다
get a seat on the
bus/subway

~에게
자리를 양보하다
give up one's seat for ~,
offer one's seat to ~

교통약자석에 앉다
sit in the
priority seat

임산부 배려석에 앉다
sit in the seat for
pregnant women

버스에서 하차
버튼을 누르다
press the STOP
button on the bus

지하철/버스/택시에
물건을 두고 내리다
leave something on the
subway/on the bus/in a taxi

내릴 정류장을
지나치다
pass a stop
to get off

SENTENCES TO USE

지하철 시간표를 미리 확인하는 게 좋다.　　It's better to check the subway schedule in advance.

우리는 버스 노선도를 확인하고 내려야 할 곳을 정했다.
We checked the bus route map and decided where to get off.

여기 오려고 버스에서 지하철로 환승했어요.　　I transferred from the bus to the subway to get here.

그 소년은 한 할머니께 자리를 양보했다.　　The boy gave up his seat for an elderly woman.

하차 버튼 좀 눌러. 우리 이번 정류장에서 내려야 해.
Press the STOP button. We have to get off at this stop.

택시를 호출하다
call a taxi
우버 택시를 부르다
call an Uber

앱으로 택시를 호출하다
call a taxi using
an app

택시를 잡다
get[catch, hail]
a taxi

기사에게 행선지를 말하다
tell one's destination
to the driver,
tell the driver where to go

(신용카드로/현금으로)
택시 요금을 지불하다
pay the taxi fare[one's taxi ride]
(by credit card/in cash)

영수증을 받다
get a receipt
거스름돈을 받다
get the change

택시 기사가 미터기를 누르다
start[turn on] the meter
택시 기사가 미터기를 끄다
turn off the meter

택시 요금 야간 할증료를 내다
pay taxi fare midnight
surcharge

(택시 기사가) 승차를 거부하다
refuse to take
a passenger

SENTENCES TO USE

요즘은 앱으로 택시를 호출할 수 있다.
These days, you can call a taxi using an app.

이 거리에서는 택시 잡기가 힘들다.
It's hard to catch a taxi on this street.

나는 너무 피곤해서 택시 기사에게 행선지를 말한 후 눈을 감았다.
I was so tired that I closed my eyes after telling the taxi driver where to go.

택시비는 신용카드로 결제했다.
I paid the taxi fare by credit card.

승차를 거부하는 택시 기사들을 가끔 본다.
Sometimes I see taxi drivers who refuse to take passengers.

Choose your SEAT

기차표/고속버스표를 끊다[사다]/예매하다
buy/book[reserve] a train ticket/
an express bus ticket

기차/고속버스의 좌석을 선택하다
choose one's seat
on the train/express bus

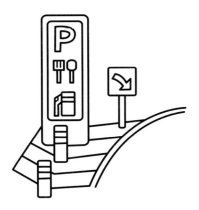

고속도로 휴게소에 들르다
stop by[at]
a highway[expressway]
rest[service] area

자전거/오토바이/전동 킥보드를 타다
ride a bicycle[bike]/
a motorcycle[motorbike]/
an electric scooter

SENTENCES TO USE

나는 늘 기차표를 모바일로 예매한다.
I always book my train tickets by mobile.

나는 표를 예매할 때 고속버스의 좌석을 선택했다.
I chose my seat on the express bus when I booked the ticket.

그는 출장 중에 고속도로 휴게소에 들러서 점심을 먹었다.
During the business trip, he stopped at the highway rest area and ate lunch.

요즘 많은 사람들이 공용 전동 킥보드를 탄다.
These days, many people ride the electric scooters from scooter-sharing programs.

비행기/배를 타다[오르다]
take a plane/ship,
get on the plane/ship

비행기/배로 ~에 가다
go to ~ by plane/ship

항공권을 예매하다
book[reserve] a[one's] flight
[plane ticket, airline ticket]

공항에서 체크인하다
check in at the
airport

짐을 부치다
check one's
baggage

금속 탐지기를 통과하다
go through
the metal detector

출국 수속을 하다
go through the departure
procedure[process]

비행기에 탑승하다
board a
flight[plane]

비행기 탑승교를 지나다
go along the passenger boarding
bridge[jet bridge, air bridge]

비행기 트랩을 오르다/내리다
go up/down
the ramp

SENTENCES TO USE

나는 배를 타고 제주도에 여행 간 적이 있다.　　I have traveled to Jeju Island by ship.

이번 가을에 뉴욕행 항공권을 예매했다.　　I booked a flight to New York this fall.

비행기 출발 2시간 전에 공항에서 체크인하는 게 좋다.
You should check in at the airport two hours before the flight is scheduled to leave.

그녀는 인공심박동기를 하고 있어서 금속탐지기를 통과할 수 없다.
She has a pacemaker, so she can't go through the metal detector.

나는 공항에서 출국 수속을 하다가 유명인을 보았다.
I saw a celebrity while going through the departure procedure at the airport.

짐을 좌석 위 짐칸에 넣다
put one's baggage[luggage] in the overhead compartment
짐을 좌석 위 짐칸에서 내리다
take one's baggage[luggage] out of the overhead compartment

좌석을 찾아서 앉다
find one's seat
and be seated

음료 서비스를 받다
get served a
beverage[drink]

기내식을 먹다
eat[have] an in-flight
meal[airline meal]

승무원에게 도움을 청하다
ask a flight attendant
for help

비행기를 갈아타다
change planes

페리를 예약하다
book[reserve]
a ferry

매표소에서
페리 표를 구매하다
buy a ferry ticket at
the ticket office

개찰구에서 승선권과
신분증을 보여 주다
show one's boarding pass
and ID at the ticket gate

자동차를 카페리에 싣다
drive one's car onto
a car ferry

SENTENCES TO USE

나는 비행기에 탄 후 좌석을 찾고 짐을 좌석 위 짐칸에 넣었다.
After getting on the plane, I found my seat and put my luggage in the overhead compartment.

나는 기내식 먹는 걸 좋아한다. 여행 갈 때만 먹을 수 있기 때문이다.
I like to eat in-flight meals because I only get to eat them when I travel.

레이캬비크로 가는 길에 런던에서 비행기를 갈아탔다.　I changed planes in London on my way to Reykjavik.

우리는 그 섬으로 가는 페리를 예약했다.　　　We booked a ferry to the island.

나는 개찰구에서 승선권과 신분증을 보여 준 다음 배에 탔다.
I showed my boarding pass and ID at the ticket gate and got on the ship.

MP3 077

운전을 배우다
learn to drive

운전 연수를 받다
take driving lessons

운전면허증을 따다[취득하다]
get[obtain] one's driver's license

운전면허증을 갱신하다
renew one's driver's license

자동차/트럭/승합차를 운전하다
drive a car/truck/van

안전띠를 착용하고 있다 (상태)
wear one's seat belt

안전띠를 매다/풀다
fasten/take off one's seat belt

직진하다
go straight

후진하다
back one's car, reverse one's car

우회전/좌회전하다
turn right/left, make a right/left

차선을 바꾸다
change lanes

U턴하다/P턴하다
make a U-turn/P-turn

사이드미러/백미러로 뒤를 보다
look back in the side mirror/rear-view mirror

~ 앞으로 끼어들다
cut in front of ~

SENTENCES TO USE

나는 스무 살 때 운전면허증을 땄다.
I got my driver's license when I was 20.

이제는 차량의 모든 좌석에서 안전띠를 매야 한다.
Now everyone in the car must wear their seat belt.

초보 운전자 시절에는 차선을 바꾸는 게 쉽지 않았다.
It was not easy to change lanes when I was a novice driver.

내비게이션에 100미터 앞에서 U턴을 하라고 나온다.
The navigation says to make a U-turn 100 meters ahead.

차 한 대가 좌회전 차선에 늘어선 다른 차량들 앞으로 끼어들었다.
A car cut in front of the other cars in the left turn lane.

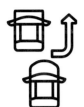
~를 추월하다
pass ~,
overtake ~

안전거리를 유지하다
maintain a safe
distance

제한 속도를 지키다
keep the speed
limit

속도를 내다
speed up,
accelerate

속도를 늦추다
slow down

제동을 걸다, 브레이크를 밟다
brake, put the brakes on,
hit the brakes(급제동을 걸다)

방향 지시등을 켜다
turn on the turn signal,
put the turn signal on

비상등을 켜다
turn on the hazard
lights[four-way flashers]

경적을 울리다
honk
the[one's]
horn

지정 차로로 달리다
drive in the designated lane
바깥쪽/안쪽 차선으로 주행하다
drive in the outside/inside lane

갓길로 달리다
drive on the shoulder

갓길에 정차하다
stop[pull over] (a car)
on the shoulder

SENTENCES TO USE

특히 고속도로에서는 안전거리를 유지하고 제한 속도를 지켜야 한다.
You have to maintain a safe distance and keep the speed limit, especially on highways.

앞차가 갑자기 멈추는 바람에 나는 급히 브레이크를 밟았다.
The car in front stopped suddenly, so I hit the brakes.

우회전이나 좌회전을 하기 전에는 방향 지시등을 켜야 한다.
You should turn on the turn signals before turning right or left.

다른 운전자에게 위험을 경고할 때만 경적을 울려야 한다.
You should only honk the horn to warn other drivers of danger.

갓길에 차를 정차하는 것은 위험하다.
It is dangerous to stop a car on the shoulder.

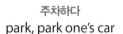

주차하다
park, park one's car

~를 태우다
pick up ~, pick ~ up

~를 내려 주다
drop ~ off

안전 운전을 하다
drive safely

교통 법규를 준수하다/위반하다
follow[obey]/violate
the traffic laws[rules]

교통 신호를 지키다
observe the
traffic signal

신호를 위반하다
run the red light, roll
through the stop sign

과속하다
speed,
be over the speed limit

속도위반으로 딱지를 떼다
get a ticket for speeding,
get a speeding ticket

SENTENCES TO USE

그녀는 학원에서 돌아오는 아들을 태우러 가야 한다.
She has to pick up her son coming back from the academy.

운전을 할 때는 교통 법규를 준수해야 한다.
When you drive, you must follow the traffic laws.

그 운전자는 교통 신호를 위반해서 사고를 냈다.
The driver ran the red light and caused the accident.

그녀는 속도 위반으로 딱지를 자주 뗀다.
She often gets speeding tickets.

졸음운전을 하다
drive drowsy, drive while tired,
fall asleep at the wheel

졸음운전
drowsy driving, tired driving

휴게소[졸음 쉼터]에서 잠깐 자다
take a nap at a rest area

견인차로 실려 가다
have one's car towed

블랙박스 영상을 확인하다
watch[view] the dash cam
[dashboard camera] videos

SENTENCES TO USE

졸음운전이 고속도로 사고의 가장 흔한 원인이다.
Drowsy driving is the most common cause of highway accidents.

나는 너무 졸려서 졸음 쉼터에서 잠깐 잤다.
I was so sleepy that I took a nap at the rest area.

자동차 시동이 걸리지 않아서 그는 차를 견인해야 했다.
His car wouldn't start and he had to have his car towed.

자동차 사고가 발생해서 우리는 블랙박스 영상을 확인했다.
As we had a car accident, we watched the dash cam video.

음주 운전을 하다
drink and drive
음주 운전
drunk driving

음주 단속에 걸리다
get caught at
a sobriety checkpoint

음주 측정기를 불다
breathe[blow] into
a breathalyzer

음주 측정을 거부하다
refuse a breathalyzer test

음주 운전으로 체포되다
be arrested for drunk
driving

면허가 정지되다
one's driver's license is suspended

면허가 취소되다
have[get] one's driver's license revoked

SENTENCES TO USE

음주 운전은 어떤 일이 있어도 절대로 하면 안 된다.
You should never drink and drive under any circumstances.

음주 측정기 불어 본 적 있어요?
Have you ever breathed into a breathalyzer?

그는 음주 운전으로 운전면허가 취소됐다.
He got his driver's license revoked for drunk driving.

교통사고가 나다
have a car accident[a traffic accident],
be in a car crash

사고 위치를 표시하다
mark the location of the accident

접촉사고를 내다
have a fender bender

(차가) 고장 나다
break down

차가 펑크 나다
have a flat tire, a tire goes flat

보험사에 연락하다
contact one's insurance company

SENTENCES TO USE

그녀는 야구 경기를 보고 오는 길에 접촉사고를 냈다.
She had a fender bender on her way back from the baseball game.

주차장에서 출발하려는데 차가 펑크 났다는 걸 알았다.
I was about to leave the parking lot when I found out that I had a flat tire.

교통사고가 나면 보험사에 연락해야 한다.
If you are in a car accident, you should contact your insurance company.

MP3 078

주유하다
put gas
in one's car

셀프 주유하다
put gas in one's
car oneself

차에 휘발유를 가득 채우다
fill up (one's car),
gas up one's car

주유구를 열다
open the fuel door

세차하다(다른 사람이)
have[get] one's
car washed

자동 세차를 하다
go through an
automatic car wash

손세차를 하다(직접)
handwash one's car,
wash one's car by hand

차를 점검하다
have[get] one's
car checked

고장 난 차를 고치다
have[get] one's car
repaired[fixed]

폐차하다
scrap
one's car

SENTENCES TO USE

나는 여행을 떠나기 전에 차에 휘발유를 가득 채웠다. I filled up my car before I left for the trip.

주유를 하려면 우선 주유구를 열어야 한다. You have to open the fuel door to put gas in your car.

나는 주유를 한 후 종종 자동 세차를 한다.
I sometimes go through an automatic car wash after putting gas in my car.

그는 자기 차를 직접 손세차한다. He handwashes his car himself.

그녀는 차가 고장 나서 카센터에 고치러 갔다.
Her car broke down so she went to the repair shop to have it repaired.

엔진오일/브레이크 오일을
점검하다/교환하다
have[get] the engine
oil/brake oil checked/
changed

워셔액을 보충하다
add[refill] washer
fluid[windshield
wiper fluid](직접)

냉각수를
보충하다/교체하다
add/change coolant
(직접), have coolant
added/changed

에어 필터를 교환하다
change one's[the]
car air filter(직접),
have one's[the] car
air filter changed

타이어를 점검하다/교환하다
have the tires
checked/rotated

휠 얼라인먼트를 받다
get a wheel alignment,
get the wheels aligned

와이퍼를 교환하다
change the wipers[windshield
wipers](직접), have the wipers
[windshield wipers] changed

에어컨을 점검하다
have the air
conditioner checked

선팅을 하다
have one's[the] car
windows tinted

진공청소기로 차량
내부를 청소하다
vacuum the interior
of one's car

바닥 매트를
청소하다
clean the
floor mats

SENTENCES TO USE

엔진오일은 1만 킬로미터 주행할 때마다 교환하는 게 좋다.
You should get the engine oil changed every 10,000 kilometers.

나는 자동차 워셔액을 직접 보충할 수 있다.　　　I can add washer fluid myself.

그녀는 작년부터 자동차의 에어 필터를 더 자주 교환하고 있다.
She's been changing her car air filter more often since last year.

나는 엔진오일을 교환할 때마다 타이어를 점검 받는다.
Every time I have my car engine oil changed, I get the tires checked.

그는 가끔 진공청소기로 차량 내부를 청소한다.　　　He sometimes vacuums the interior of his car.

CHAPTER

8

SOCIETY & POLITICS

1 사고, 재해

MP3 **0 7 9**

교통사고가 나다
have a car accident,
be in a car crash

접촉사고가 나다
have a fender
bender

차에 치이다
be hit[be run
over] by a car

열차가 탈선하다
a train derails[is
derailed]

비행기가 추락하다
an airplane
crashes

배가 침몰하다
a ship sinks

지하철에서 화재가 발생하다
a fire breaks out in[on]
the subway

화재가 발생하다
a fire breaks out

건물이 붕괴되다
a building collapses

무너진 건물에 갇히다
be trapped under
a collapsed building

폭발 사고가 일어나다
an explosion occurs

가스 폭발 사고
a gas explosion

SENTENCES TO USE

오늘 퇴근길에 가벼운 접촉사고가 났다.
I had a minor fender bender on my way home from work today.

그 배달원은 음식을 배달하던 중에 차에 치였다. The delivery man was hit by a car while delivering food.

오늘 그 도시에서 열차가 탈선해서 많은 사람이 다쳤다.
Many people were injured today when a train derailed in the city.

비행기가 추락하면 흔히 많은 탑승객들이 목숨을 잃는다.
Often, when an airplane crashes, many of the passengers lose their lives.

지하철에서 화재가 발생하면 큰 인명 사고로 이어질 수 있다.
If a fire breaks out on the subway, it can lead to a mass mortality event.

화상을 입다
get burned,
burn oneself,
get a burn

1도/2도/3도 화상을 입다
get a first-degree/
second-degree/
third-degree burn

전신 화상을 입다
burn oneself
all over

물에 빠지다
fall into
the water

익사하다
drown

공사 현장/아파트 베란다/
건물 옥상
…에서 추락하다
fall from[off]
a construction site/
an apartment balcony/
a building rooftop …

근무 중에
다치다/사망하다
get injured/die
at work[on duty]

산업 재해를
당하다
suffer an
industrial injury

과로사하다
work oneself
to death

외상후스트레스증후군
(PTSD)에 시달리다
suffer from PTSD(post-
traumatic stress disorder)

의료 사고가 발생하다
a medical accident
occurs

구급차를 부르다
call
an ambulance

응급실에 실려 가다
be taken to the ER
(emergency room)

SENTENCES TO USE

나는 어렸을 때 뜨거운 물에 화상을 입은 적이 있다. I once got burned by hot water when I was young.

그 사고로 몇 명이 강물에 빠져 익사했다. Several people drowned in the river in the accident.

근무 중 다치는 사람들에 대한 보상이 제대로 이루어져야 한다.
Compensation for people who get injured on duty should be done properly.

지금은 의료 사고가 발생했을 때 환자가 그것을 입증해야 한다.
Now, when a medical accident occurs, the patient has to prove it.

사람들이 구급차를 불렀고, 그 남자는 응급실에 실려 갔다.
People called an ambulance, and the man was taken to the ER.

사람이 자연 재해를 겪다
experience[live through]
a natural disaster,
be hit[struck] by a natural disaster

지역이 자연 재해를 입다
suffer (from) a natural disaster,
be hit[struck] by a natural disaster

사람이 폭우/홍수로 피해를 입다
be affected by heavy rain/flood

지역이 폭우/홍수로 피해를 입다/파괴되다/황폐화되다
be affected by[suffer from]/be destroyed by/
be devastated by heavy rain/flood

사물이 폭우/홍수로 피해를 입다
be damaged by heavy rain/flood

사람이 태풍으로 피해를 입다
be hit by[be affected by] a typhoon

지역이 태풍으로 피해를 입다/파괴되다/
황폐화되다
be hit by[be affected by]/
be destroyed by/be devastated by
a typhoon

사물이 태풍으로 피해를 입다
be damaged by a typhoon

사람이 폭염으로 고생하다
be caught in
[be affected by]
a heat wave

지역이 폭염으로
피해를 입다
be affected by
[suffer from] a heat
wave

사람이 한파로 고생하다
be caught in
[be affected by]
a cold wave

지역이 한파로 피해를 입다
be affected by
[suffer from]
a cold wave

사람이 폭설로 피해를 입다
be affected by heavy snow

지역이 폭설로 피해를 입다
be affected by[suffer from]
heavy snow

사람이 눈사태/산사태로 피해를 입다
be caught in[be affected by] an
avalanche/a landslide

지역이 눈사태/산사태로 피해를 입다/파괴되다
be affected by[suffer from]/be
destroyed by an avalanche/a landslide

사람이 가뭄으로 고생하다
be affected by drought

지역이 가뭄으로 피해를 입다
suffer from[be affected by] drought

사람이 산불로 피해를 입다
be affected by a forest fire

지역이나 사물이 산불로 피해를 입다/파괴되다
be affected by/be destroyed by a forest fire

사람이 지진으로/지진 해일로 피해를 입다
be affected by an earthquake/a tsunami

지역이 지진으로/지진 해일로 피해를 입다/파괴되다/황폐화되다
be affected by/be destroyed by/be devastated by
an earthquake/a tsunami

사물이 지진으로/지진 해일로 피해를 입다
be damaged by an earthquake/a tsunami

사람이 화산 폭발로 피해를 입다
be affected by a volcanic
eruption

지역이 화산 폭발로 피해를 입다/
파괴되다
be affected by/be destroyed
by a volcanic eruption

사람이 황사/미세먼지로 고생하다
be affected by yellow dust/fine dust

지역이 황사/미세먼지로 피해를 입다
be affected by[suffer from] yellow dust/
fine dust

사람이 싱크홀로 피해를 입다
be affected by a sinkhole

지역이 싱크홀로 피해를 입다/파괴되다
be affected by/be destroyed
by a sinkhole

SENTENCES TO USE

그 마을은 이번 폭우로 큰 피해를 입었다.
The village was badly damaged by this heavy rain.

수많은 사람들이 그 지진으로 피해를 입었다.
Hundreds of people were affected by the earthquake.

MP3 080

범죄를 저지르다
commit a crime

도망치다
flee, run away

체포되다
be[get] arrested

~를 훔치다
steal ~

A에게서 B를 훔치다
rob A of B

소매치기를 하다
pickpocket

사기를 치다
commit fraud,
con, swindle

~짜리 지폐를 위조하다
counterfeit a ~ bill

불법 도박을 하다
do illegal
gambling

~에게 뇌물을 주다
bribe ~, give[offer]
a bribe to ~

~를 횡령하다
embezzle ~

보이스피싱으로 사기를 치다
commit fraud
with voice phishing

SENTENCES TO USE

그 남자는 범죄를 저지르고 도망쳤다.
The man committed a crime and ran away.

그 상점은 카운터에 있는 현금을 모두 도둑맞았다.
The store was robbed of all the cash on the counter.

그 코미디언은 불법 도박으로 TV 출연이 정지되었다.
The comedian was suspended from appearing on TV for illegal gambling.

그 무기상은 국방 업무와 관련 있는 정치가들에게 뇌물을 주었다.
The arms dealer bribed politicians involved in defense.

보이스피싱으로 사기를 치는 인간들이 요즘도 여전히 많다.
There are still many people who commit fraud with voice phishing these days.

사이버 범죄를 저지르다
commit cyber crime

명예를 훼손하다
harm[damage, defame]
someone's reputation

업무상 기밀을 누설하다
leak[reveal, give away] company
confidential information

공무 집행을 방해하다
obstruct the execution of official duties, interfere
with a public official in the execution of his/her duty

무고하다
make a false
accusation,
falsely accuse

사문서를 위조하다
forge a private
document

~를 표절하다
plagiarize ~

음주 운전을 하다
drink and drive

무면허 운전을 하다
drive without
a license

보복 운전을 하다
have road rage

뺑소니를 치다
hit and run

SENTENCES TO USE

그 유튜버는 한 여성 배우의 명예를 훼손한 데 대해 유죄 판결을 받았다.
The YouTuber was found guilty of defaming an actress's reputation.

그는 공무 집행을 방해한 혐의로 벌금형에 처해졌다.
He was fined for obstructing the execution of official duties.

그 여성은 상대 남성을 성폭행 혐의로 무고한 것으로 드러났다.
The woman was found to have falsely accused the other man of sexual assault.

그 베스트셀러 작가는 덜 인기 있는 책을 표절한 것으로 의심받았다.
The author of the best seller was suspected of plagiarizing a less popular book.

그 남성은 무면허 운전을 하다가 경찰에 잡혔다.
The man was caught driving without a license by the police.

마약을 복용하다
take drugs

마약을 밀수하다
smuggle drugs

~를 폭행하다
hit ~, assault ~

성범죄를 저지르다
commit a sex crime

성희롱하다
sexually
harass

성추행하다
indecently assault,
molest

성폭행하다
sexually assault,
rape

데이트 폭력을 저지르다
commit dating violence,
physically assault ~ while dating

성매매를 하다
pay for sex,
prostitute (매춘부로 일하다)

몰카를 촬영하다
secretly record
videos

스토킹하다
stalk

SENTENCES TO USE

그 남자는 마약을 복용하고 밀수한 혐의로 재판에 넘겨졌다.
The man was put on trial on charges of taking drugs and smuggling them.

그 정치가는 성범죄를 저지른 탓에 정치 인생이 끝났다.
The politician's political life ended because he committed a sex crime.

데이트 폭력을 저지르는 것은 대부분 남성들이지만 가끔 여성이 저지르기도 한다.
It's mostly men who commit dating violence, but sometimes women commit it, too.

그 가수는 몰카 촬영 및 유포 혐의로 실형을 선고받았다.
The singer was sentenced to prison for secretly recording videos and distributing them.

스토킹에 대한 처벌이 강화되어야 한다는 의견이 지배적이다.
The prevailing view is that the punishment for stalking should be increased.

~를 납치하다, 유괴하다
kidnap ~

~를 인신매매하다
traffic in ~

아동/노인/동물을 학대하다
abuse[mistreat] a child/
an old man/an animal

~를 살해하다
murder ~, kill ~

살인 미수에 그치다
the attempt to
murder has failed

연쇄 살인을 저지르다
commit serial
murders

연쇄 살인범
a serial killer

사체를 유기하다
dump a body

~에 방화하다, 불을 지르다
set ~ on fire,
set fire to ~

테러를 저지르다
commit an act
of terrorism

자살 폭탄 테러를 하다
carry out a suicide
bombing

SENTENCES TO USE

예전에 교사가 자신의 제자를 유괴, 살해하는 사건이 있었다.
In the past, there was an incident in which a teacher kidnapped and killed his student.

동물을 학대하는 사람은 사람도 학대하기 쉽다.　　People who abuse animals are likely to abuse people.

그 남자는 5년 동안 10명을 죽였다. 즉, 연쇄 살인범이었다.
The man killed 10 people in five years. In other words, he was a serial killer.

한 술 취한 사람이 한밤중에 그 문에 불을 질렀다.
A drunk man set the gate on fire in the middle of the night.

그 테러리스트는 자살 폭탄 테러를 저질렀다.　　The terrorist carried out a suicide bombing.

MP3 081

법을 지키다
observe[abide by] the law
법을 어기다
break[violate] the law

~를 고소하다, 고발하다
accuse ~, sue ~
~를 기소하다
indict ~
~를 대상으로 민사 소송을 제기하다
file a civil suit[lawsuit] against ~
~를 대상으로 형사 소송을 제기하다
file a criminal suit against ~

~에게 이혼 소송을 제기하다
file for divorce from ~

재판하다
try

변론하다
plead, defend

증언하다
give testimony

검사가 ~를 구형하다
the prosecutor
demands[asks for] ~

판결을 내리다
judge

유죄 판결/
무죄 판결을 받다
be found guilty/not guilty

SENTENCES TO USE

법은 최대한 지켜야 한다.
You must abide by the law as much as possible.

그 가수는 악플러들을 고소했다.
The singer sued Internet trolls.

그 여성은 자기 남편에게 이혼 소송을 제기했다.
The woman filed for divorce from her husband.

검사는 피고에게 징역 7년을 구형했다.
The prosecutor demanded a seven-year prison term for the defendant.

그 사람은 5년간의 재판 끝에 결국 무죄 판결을 받았다.
The man was eventually found not guilty after a trial that lasted five years.

형을 선고하다
sentence
~년 형/무기징역/사형을 선고 받다
be sentenced to ~ years in prison/life in prison/death
집행유예를 선고 받다
be sentenced to probation

벌금형을 받다
be fined,
be sentenced to a fine

구치소/교도소에
수감되다, 감옥에 가다
go to jail/prison, be sent
to[be put into] jail/prison

~ 동안 복역하다
serve ~ in prison

독방에 수감되다
be put into solitary confinement

보석을 신청하다
apply for bail
보석금을 내고 석방되다
be released on bail

~로 감형되다
be reduced [commuted] to ~

(모범수로) 가석방되다
be paroled, be released on parole (because he/she is a model prisoner)

사면 받다
be pardoned

(상급 법원에)
상소하다, 항소하다
appeal
(to a higher court)

SENTENCES TO USE

재판부는 자신의 딸을 방치하여 숨지게 한 여성에게 20년 형을 선고했다.
The court sentenced the woman to 20 years in prison for child neglect leading to the death of her daughter.

그는 음주 운전으로 벌금형을 선고받았다.　　He was fined for drunk driving.

그는 감옥에서 12년을 복역했고, 출소 직후 또 범죄를 저질렀다.
He served 12 years in prison and committed another crime right after he was released.

그 재소자는 복역 10년 만에 모범수로 가석방되었다.
The prisoner was released on parole after 10 years in prison because he had been a model prisoner.

그녀는 유죄 판결을 받았지만 곧바로 항소했다.　　She was found guilty but appealed immediately.

투표하다
vote

선거로 ~를 뽑다
elect ~

선거를 실시하다
hold an election

대통령 선거를 실시하다
hold a presidential
election

국회의원 선거를 실시하다
hold legislative[parliamentary] elections

지자체장 선거를 실시하다
hold local government elections

재선거/보궐 선거를 실시하다
hold reelections/
by-elections

사전 투표를 하다
vote in advance of
the election day

사전 투표
early voting

투표에 기권하다
abstain from voting

~(후보)에게 투표하다
vote for ~

투표용지에 기표하다
fill out[in] a ballot

투표용지를 투표함에 넣다
put a ballot in
a ballot box

투표 인증 사진을 찍다
take photos as proof
of voting

SENTENCES TO USE

투표를 하는 것은 민주주의 국가 국민의 권리이자 의무다.
It is the right and duty of the people of a democratic country to vote.

대통령 직선제에서는 국민이 대통령을 직접 뽑는다.
In the direct presidential election system, the people directly elect the president.

그 나라에서는 대통령 선거는 5년마다 실시하고 국회의원 선거는 4년마다 실시한다.
In the country, presidential elections are held every five years and legislative elections are held every four years.

지난달에 우리 시는 시장 보궐 선거를 실시했다.
Last month, our city held a by-election for mayor.

나는 사전 투표를 했다.
I voted in advance of the election day.

대통령에 출마하다
run for the presidency, run for president
국회의원에 출마하다
run for a seat in the National Assembly
시장에 출마하다
run for mayor
후보자로 등록하다
register as a candidate

Election

재선에 불출마하다
not seek
re-election

후보자를 지지하다
support
a candidate

선거 운동을 하다
campaign for election,
go on a campaign

여론 조사를 하다
conduct
a (public opinion) poll

여론 조사에 응하다
respond to
a (public opinion) poll

개표하다
count votes

선거 결과를 발표하다
announce the result
of the election

선거에서 이기다/지다
win/lose an
election

당선증을 받다
receive a certificate
of election

SENTENCES TO USE

그 배우는 전에 국회의원에 출마했다.
The actor ran for a seat in the National Assembly before.

그 국회의원은 재선 불출마를 선언했다.
The lawmaker announced he was not seeking re-election.

너는 지지하는 후보가 있니?   Is there a candidate you are going to support?

오늘 나는 다가오는 대통령 선거에 대한 여론조사에 응했다.
Today I responded to a poll about the upcoming presidential election.

그 선거구에서는 선거가 끝나고 1시간 뒤에 개표를 시작했다.
The election district began counting votes an hour after the election was over.

MP3 083

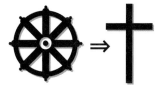

(종교)를 믿다
believe in ~

성당/교회/절에 다니다
go to Catholic church/church/Buddhist temple

~로 개종하다
convert to ~

천주교

(성당에서)
미사를 드리다
go to mass

온라인으로 미사를 드리다
attend mass online

기도하다
pray

묵주 기도를 드리다
pray the rosary

강론을 듣다
listen to the
sermon

성호를 긋다
cross oneself

SENTENCES TO USE

그 여성은 남편의 종교인 개신교로 개종해서 교회에서 결혼할 수 있었다.
The woman converted to her husband's religion, Protestantism, so they could be married in the church.

그는 매주 일요일에 미사를 드린다.
He goes to mass every Sunday.

그녀는 식사를 하기 전이면 늘 성호를 긋는다.
She always crosses herself before eating meals.

미사포를 쓰다
wear a veil

세례명을 정하다
decide on a baptismal
name[Christian name]

세례를 받다
be baptized

고해성사를 하다
go to confession,
confess (one's sins)

영성체를 하다
take communion

대부/대모가 되다
become a godfather/
godmother

SENTENCES TO USE

여성 신도들은 성당에서 미사포를 쓰고 기도를 한다.
Female believers pray in the cathedral wearing veils.

우리 엄마는 60대에 천주교 세례를 받았다.
My mother was baptized a Catholic in her sixties.

네가 천주교 신자라면 신부님께 모든 걸 다 고해성사를 하겠니?
If you were a Catholic, would you confess everything to a priest?

개신교

교회에 가다, 교회에 다니다
go to church,
attend church

예배에 참석하다
attend a service

새벽 예배에 가다
attend an early
morning service

가정 예배를 드리다
hold[give] family
worship

온라인으로 예배를 드리다
attend online worship service

구역 예배를 보다
have a district service,
have a service with the same
district group

찬송가를 부르다
sing a hymn

설교를 듣다
listen to
the sermon

헌금을 내다
give an offering,
make an offering of money

SENTENCES TO USE

나는 중학교 때 몇 달간 교회에 다녔다.
I attended church for several months when I was in middle school.

코로나19 때문에 요즘 우리는 온라인으로 예배를 드린다.
Because of COVID-19, we attend online services these days.

나는 예배 중에 찬송가 부르는 게 제일 좋다.
I like singing hymns during the services most of all.

십일조를 내다
give tithes, tithe

교리 교육을 받다
take a baptism class

주일학교 선생님을 하다
be a Sunday school
teacher

부흥회에 참석하다
attend a revival
meeting[assembly]

전도하다
evangelize

성경을 읽다/필사하다
read/transcribe
the Bible

QT 시간을 갖다
have a quiet[Bible] time

성경 공부를 하다
study the Bible,
participate in a Bible study group

SENTENCES TO USE

그는 매달 십일조를 낸다.
He gives tithes every month.

그녀는 몇 년 전부터 주일학교 선생님을 해 왔다.
She has been a Sunday school teacher for several years.

나는 요즘 성경을 매일 한 시간씩 필사한다.
I transcribe the Bible for an hour every day these days.

불교

예불을 드리다
attend a Buddhist service

불공드리다
pray to Buddha, offer a Buddhist prayer, worship in the Buddhist temple

합장하다
put one's hands together in front of the chest [as if in prayer]

염주를 돌리며 기도하다
count one's beads

불경을 (소리 내어) 읽다
read the Buddhist scriptures (out loud)

절을 하다   108배를 하다
make   make one hundred
a deep bow   and eight bows

설법을 듣다
listen to the monk's sermon

시주하다
give alms, donate[offer] money/rice/a building/ property ...

향을 피우다, 분향하다
burn incense

촛불을 밝히다
light a candle

연등에 불을 밝히다
light a lotus lantern

SENTENCES TO USE

그 여성은 자식들을 위해 불공을 드린다.
The woman prays to Buddha for her children.

승려가 눈을 감고 앉아 염주를 돌리며 기도하고 있었다.
The monk was counting his beads while sitting with his eyes closed.

불자들이 불경을 소리 내어 읽고 있었다.
The Buddhists were reading the Buddhist scriptures out loud.

그녀는 매일 아침 108배를 한다.
She makes one hundred and eight bows every morning.

나는 자기 전에 유튜브로 스님들의 설법을 듣는다.
I listen to monks' sermons on YouTube before I go to bed.

6 군대

MP3 **084**

군대에 가다, 입대하다
join the military,
enlist (in ~)

육군/해군/공군/해병대에 입대하다
enlist in the army/navy/
air force/marine corps

군복무하다
serve in the military,
do one's military service

신체검사를 받다
get[receive] a physical
examination

신병 훈련을 받다
do boot camp, receive
basic training at boot camp

자대 배치를 받다
be assigned to a unit

경례하다
salute,
give a salute

군번줄을 착용하다
wear dog tags

점호하다
take[make, have]
a roll call

SENTENCES TO USE

그들은 군에 입대하여 1개월 동안 신병 훈련소로 보내졌다.
After joining the military, they were sent to boot camp for one month.

그 가수는 5월 말에 입대했다.
The singer enlisted at the end of May.

우리 아버지는 38개월 동안 군복무를 하셨다.
My father served in the military for 38 months.

그들은 신병 훈련소에서 기본 훈련을 받은 후에 자대 배치를 받았다.
They were assigned to units after receiving basic training at boot camp.

행군하다
march

구보하다
march at double-quick

보초를 서다
mount guard, stand sentry,
stand guard

불침번을 서다
keep a night watch

관등성명을 대다
give one's name, rank,
and serial number

12:00 AM

야간 훈련을 하다
do[take part in] night training
[nighttime training]

SENTENCES TO USE

여름에 주간 행군은 정말 힘들다.
It's really hard to march during the day in summer.

군인 둘이 탄약고 앞에서 보초를 서고 있었다.
Two soldiers were standing guard in front of the ammunition depot.

그는 새벽 12시부터 3시까지 불침번을 섰다.
He kept a night watch from 12 a.m. to 3 a.m.

그 부대는 올해부터 야간 훈련을 실시하기 시작했다.
The unit began doing night training this year.

동계/하계 훈련을 하다
do[take part in] winter/summer training

유격 훈련을 하다
do[take part in] guerrilla training

군가를 부르다
sing a military song[war song]

위문편지를 받다
receive a letter of consolation

면회를 오다
visit, come to visit

휴가를 나가다/휴가 중이다
go/be on leave

부대에 복귀하다
return to one's unit

재난 지역에서 구호 활동을 하다
take part in relief work in disaster areas

군부대 위문 공연을 즐기다
enjoy the show at a military camp

군병원으로 후송되다
be taken to a military hospital

제대하다
be discharged (from the military service)

탈영하다
go AWOL(absent without leave), desert[run away]
from the army[military]

영창에 가다
be confined[locked up] in the guardhouse

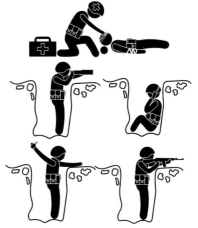

SENTENCES TO USE

우리는 4박 5일 동안 유격 훈련을 했다.
We did guerrilla training for four nights and five days.

지난 주말에 여자 친구가 부대로 나를 면회 왔다.
Last weekend, my girlfriend came to visit me at my unit.

내일은 그가 휴가 중이었다가 부대에 복귀하는 날이다.
Tomorrow is the day he returns to his unit after being on leave.

그는 다음 달에 제대할 예정이다.
He is scheduled to be discharged next month.

한 남성은 군에서 탈영했다가 20년 만에 자수했다고 한다.
A man reportedly deserted from the military and turned himself in after 20 years.

INDEX 색인 찾아보기

한글 인덱스

ㄱ

ㅃ

ㅅ

ㅆ

ㅇ

ㅉㅉ

ㅎ

기타

INDEX  색인 찾아보기

영어 인덱스

M

P

T

U

V

X

Y

Z